WE ALL JUST
BOUGHT A TEAM

THE BIGGEST WHAT-IFS IN BUFFALO SPORTS HISTORY

Jeff Dahlberg

NFB Publishing
Buffalo, New York

This book is dedicated to all of Buffalo's patient, loyal and long-suffering sports fans. All of the people who tailgate at Bills games, all of the crowds who party at the Plaza and get hopeful every September and October. May your loyalty someday pay off.

WE ALL JUST BOUGHT A TEAM

CONTENTS

INTRODUCTION

ONE SPRING MORNING in 2018, I happened to catch Mike Pesca promoting a new book on TV called Upon Further Review: The Greatest What-Ifs in Sports History. I was intrigued by the premise and almost couldn't wait to get my hands on a copy. Since my birthday was about four weeks away, I told my family it would make a great gift. When I finally did read the book a month later, I was a little disappointed. Pesca had picked a variety of sportswriters to write a chapter each on their take of the greatest what-ifs in sports history. However, astonishingly, of the 37 chapters in the book, there was not one Buffalo sports what-if. No Eichel Tank. No No Goal. No L.A. or Toronto Bills. No Wide Right.

It was another example of Buffalo being an afterthought. Western New Yorkers are used to being overlooked, that is when the national media isn't making a giant deal out of the area occasionally getting a lake effect snowstorm. Meanwhile, New York City and Boston get nor'easters that blow up the Atlantic Coast like clockwork every few years, yet no one holds it against these places or questions why anyone would want to live there. Local residents and organizations have made great strides in recent years, restoring Buffalo's stock of historic architecture, opening parks and attractions along the waterfront and trying to build a culture of entrepreneurship and business startups. The area is far from perfect but anyone who pays attention has noticed Buffalo is light years ahead of the way it was 10, 15 or 20 years ago.

We're used to being ignored, which I suppose is better than being scrutinized in a negative way. Since nobody else in the literary world thought Buffalo deserved any sports what-if mentions, I decided to tackle the topic. Buffalo has some of the greatest sports what-ifs of any city and fan base in the United States. No other NFL team can claim that it went to the Super Bowl four years in a row and unfortunately didn't win, like the Buffalo Bills in the early 1990s. Hockey fans who think they've been robbed should look at Game 6 of the 1999 Stanley Cup Finals, when Dallas Stars winger Brett Hull shot the game winning goal after he put his foot in the goal crease, even though it was against NHL rules. Recently, New York Post sports columnist Mike Vaccaro congratulated Buffalo on hosting the Toronto Blue Jays for their shortened season in August and September 2020. Vaccaro pointed out that it was the first time the city would have major league baseball games since the Federal League folded in 1915. Yes, Buffalo once had a major league ball club, more than once, in fact. The Queen City even boasted an NBA team, the Buffalo Braves, who shared space with the Sabres in downtown's Memorial Auditorium from 1970-78.

More recently, Buffalo dodged a bullet when Sabres owners Terry and Kim Pegula bought the Bills from late owner Ralph Wilson's estate when Wilson passed away in 2014. Without the Pegula's deep pockets, Buffalo could have gone the way of St. Louis, Oakland and San Diego. All three cities lost their NFL teams in recent years, when the Rams and Chargers left St. Louis and San Diego for L.A. and Oakland went to Vegas. Donald Trump and Jon Bon Jovi were the two other bidders for the Bills. Trump later said that if he had bought the Bills, he wouldn't have run for president in 2016. Think about that possibility. Bon Jovi teamed up with a Toronto business group, Maple Leaf Sports and Entertainment, which wanted to move the franchise to Canada's largest metropolis. How would our relationship with our neighbors to the north have played out if Toronto stole Buffalo's football team?

Readers can find all of these scenarios and more in these pages. Each chapter opens with a recap of what actually happened, then pivots to what could have turned out differently. The opening stories in every chapter include research on the actual events, so readers who weren't there or don't remember all the details can get a brief refresher. Different sportswriters, authors, historians, bloggers and former team personnel then discuss their view of each question. I like to compare it to a group of people talking about sports at a bar or a party and everyone is weighing in with their opinion. The result makes for a lively debate and an interesting read.

Commentators such as author and Bills historian Jeff Miller, former Buffalo News sports reporter Tim Graham, Buffalo News sportswriter Milt Northrop, Rochester Democrat and Chronicle sports reporter Sal Maiorana, former Sabres Public Relations Director Paul Wieland, Buffalo Fan Alliance President Matt Sabuda, sportswriter Chris Ostrander, hockey writer John Krieger, hockey author Ross Brewitt and Buffalo Braves historian Tim Wendel all offer fascinating, insightful, opinionated and sometimes polar opposite takes on each of the 10 biggest what-if questions in Buffalo sports history.

Readers may not agree with each person's opinion, and they may not agree with mine. But it'll give Buffalo sports fans something to think about, something to talk about and something to reminisce about. I hope you'll enjoy reading it as much as I enjoyed writing it.

Jeff Dahlberg
Tonawanda, NY
2020

CHAPTER 1
What if Terry and Kim Pegula Didn't Buy the Buffalo Bills?

In 2014, RALPH WILSON, the Buffalo Bills' owner since the team's AFL inception, passed away at the age of 95. Buffalo was in danger of losing its football franchise, the same way the St. Louis Rams left for Los Angeles. A year earlier, in 2013, St. Louis Rams owner Stan Kroenke was enjoying success in Missouri. He had a loyal fan base in a mid-sized Midwestern city. Since relocating from L.A. in the mid-1990s, the Rams had made three Super Bowl appearances and won one.[1] The team had had some losing seasons, but fans continued to support them. Elected officials promised to give Kroenke $400 million to help build a new stadium for the Rams.[2] But Kroenke wasn't satisfied. Opportunity beckoned out west, where Los Angeles wanted one of its NFL teams back. Even so, L.A. fans had the reputation of being fickle, while fans in St. Louis stuck with their franchise. In fact, both the L.A. Raiders and Rams had left the City of Angels because game day attendance wasn't high enough.[3] There were stronger fan followings in smaller cities in America's heartland.

In spite of this, Kroenke coveted the idea of building a privately financed stadium in L.A., where the corporate sponsorships and luxury seat boxes would bring in more revenue. He kept his plans a secret from the St. Louis media and the team's loyal fan base. Three years earlier, after buying majority ownership in the team, he had reassured worried Rams fans that "I'm going to attempt to do everything that I can to keep the Rams in St. Louis."[4] Kroenke added that "I've always stepped up for pro football in St. Louis. And I'm stepping up one more time. I'm born and raised in Missouri. People know I can be trusted. People know I'm an honorable guy."[5] Kroenke's Chief Operating Officer Kevin Demoff said that "our goal is to build a winner in St. Louis not only in 2012, but in 2022, 2032 and beyond."[6] If Stan Kroenke was honorable and meant what he said in 2010, by 2013 he was out in the Los Angeles area scouting sites for a new football stadium. That summer Demoff got an early morning phone call from his boss. Kroenke was ecstatic, and he told his chief operating officer he had found a property in Inglewood, California that was "an unbelievable site"[7] for a stadium.

While Kroenke was quietly maneuvering to move the St. Louis Rams back to L.A., the general consensus among sportswriters, industry prognosticators and politicians was that Los Angeles wasn't getting an NFL team anytime soon. Los Angeles City Councilman Bernard Parks despaired of L.A. landing a football franchise and openly lamented that "I've finally, personally come to a conclusion. I have to resign myself to the fact the NFL is not coming."[8] As late as 2015, even after the media had announced Kroenke's purchase of a stadium site in southern California, reporters in Los Angeles didn't believe it. Nathan Fenno and Sam Farmer of the L.A. Times wrote that "L.A. has been more valuable to the NFL without a team than with one, and owners have used the threat of moving here to improve aging stadiums and bolster bottom lines."[9]

In early 2016, NFL owners voted 30-2 to approve the St. Louis Rams' application to immediately move to Los Angeles, before Kroenke even had a new stadium up and running. The San Diego Chargers had a first option to join the Rams in the country's second largest city. Stan Kroenke's duplicity, after promising St. Louis fans that the Rams would stay in Missouri, angered the community. Kitty Ratcliffe, president of the St. Louis Convention and Visitor's Commission, said that "I... feel sorry for the fans. There are people in this community whose loyalty got crushed by an owner who never cared for them the way they cared for the team."[10] St. Louis Mayor Francis Slay blamed the NFL for letting Kroenke get away with it. "The NFL ignored the facts, the loyalty of St. Louis fans, who supported the team through more downs than ups, and the NFL ignored a strong market and a viable plan for a new stadium."[11]

NFL Commissioner Roger Goodell offered both the Rams and Chargers $100 million in league money if they stayed in St. Louis and San Diego, respectively. Goodell admitted that "Relocation is a painful process. It's painful for the fans, the communities, the teams, for the league in general. Stability is something that we've taken a great deal of pride in and in some ways a bittersweet moment because we were unsuccessful in being able to get the kind of facilities we wanted to get done in their home markets."[12] Even though Goodell claimed he wanted stability, the NFL approved three moves in less than two years. The Rams and Chargers both moved to L.A. in 2016. In 2017, after voters refused to pay for a new stadium, the Oakland Raiders announced a move to Las Vegas, where they got a new $750 million stadium on the taxpayers' dime.[13]

If not for fate, luck, circumstances, the guiding hand of football providence, Buffalo could have been the fourth unfortunate city to lose its NFL team. On March 25, 2014, longtime Bills patriarch Ralph Wilson, the only owner the team ever had since Wilson started the Bills as an AFL franchise in 1959, passed away. Almost everyone in Western New York assumed that Wilson's heirs would sell the team to an out-of-town owner who would promptly move it. Wilson had put his will into a private trust, and nervous Bills fans waited anxiously to find out who would bid for the franchise that spring and summer. By late July three contenders had emerged, Buffalo Sabres owners Terry and Kim Pegula, New York City real estate developer Donald Trump, and a Toronto ownership group headed by New Jersey rock star front man Jon Bon Jovi.[14]

The Pegulas said nothing publicly about their interest in the team, which was wise since all the bidders had signed a non-disclosure agreement not to talk about it. One of the other two bidders, however, couldn't shut up about his interest. Donald Trump tweeted that "I am the only potential owner of the@buffalo bills who will keep the team in Buffalo, where it belongs!"[15] Jon Bon Jovi and the Toronto tycoons he was in cahoots with tried to quietly keep their eyes on the prize, but local fans didn't trust their intentions. Donald Trump secretly hired Republican political operative Michael Caputo to stoke that mistrust and discredit the Toronto bidders so that he could more easily buy the team. Caputo helped form a local group called 12th Man Thunder, later Bills Fan Thunder, to organize a Bon Jovi boycott. "Trump knew he couldn't outbid the Canadians"[16] Caputo told GQ writer Ben Schrenkinger. Instead, Trump wanted Caputo to turn the Bills Mafia against the Toronto business moguls.

New Buffalo Bills owners Terry and Kim Pegula and their family at Ralph Wilson Stadium (now Bills Stadium) shortly after buying the Bills franchise in 2014. The Pegulas paid $1.4 billion for the team and outbid real estate developer Donald Trump and a Toronto business group headed by musician Jon Bon Jovi. *Photo by Craig Melvin, courtesy of Buffalo Bills LLC.*

Caputo wasted little time recruiting a group of Bills fans who would be the public face of the group. "I had it all set up with neighborhood guys who lived by the stadium"[17] he said. One of these neighborhood guys was Chuck Sonntag, a double amputee cancer survivor, who acted as the group leader. Trump soon dropped out of being involved with Bills Fan Thunder, after he signed a non-disclosure agreement to buy the Bills and had to stop publicly disclosing his interest. He told Caputo to go ahead without him, and Bills Fan Thunder did. Caputo said that "We immediately made it far more aggressive and anti-Toronto than the president ever envisioned, mostly because we didn't have to worry about getting him crossways with the NFL."[18] Even though Trump was out of it, nobody could tell anyone that he'd ever been in it. Chuck Pellien, who co-founded the group, wanted to let people know about Trump's involvement, but he and the other members had to keep that information secret. "It was all behind the scenes and we weren't even allowed to mention his name because of the agreement that he signed."[19]

Bills Fan Thunder went to work setting up "Bon Jovi Free Zones" in local bars and restaurants, and got them to refuse to play his songs. They gathered thousands of signatures for a petition to keep the Bills in Buffalo. Transit Bar and Restaurant owner Ryan Jagiello told local TV station WGRZ that banning Bon Jovi's music was an easy decision. "I wasn't a Bon Jovi fan anyways to begin with, so it's really no big deal for me not to play his music in here. I've told these bands, no, don't even think about playing it. Just take it right off your set list. He can live on a prayer somewhere else."[20] Bills Fan Thunder posted on their Facebook page that if Bon Jovi bought the Bills, "He won't be wanted dead or alive. He will be dead."[21]

Bon Jovi's efforts to reassure Bills fans that he would keep the Bills in Buffalo fell flat. Bon Jovi tried to counter the blow back by sending his friend, former quarterback and Western New York native Ron Jaworski out to tell the news media that the rock star front man wouldn't move the Bills out of Buffalo.[22] However, Toronto Sun reporter Jon Kryk disputed this, and he insisted Bon Jovi had a plan to eventually move the team to Toronto. Mike Florio of NBC Sports wrote that "For the Bills, the opportunity (to move the team) arises after the 2019 season, with a one-year out in the current lease at Ralph Wilson Stadium. If the Bills eventually will be moved, it makes sense for the owner to deny, deny and deny again any intention to move the team until the move can happen. Then, intentions suddenly will change, with some sort of cockamamie…excuse being provided for the dramatic shift in the plans for the franchise."[23]

Jon Bon Jovi responded to these accusations by repeatedly denying, denying and denying that he would move the team. On August 3rd, he wrote an open letter that The Buffalo News published. In "Why We're Bidding on the Buffalo Bills" Bon Jovi sounded very much like Stan Kroenke. He promised anxious and suspicious Bills fans that "our objective is simple: to carry on the legacy of Ralph Wilson and make the Bills successful in Buffalo."[24] If Bon Jovi thought the letter would turn skeptics into believers and smooth things over, he was deeply mistaken. Few people in Buffalo believed his reassurances. Buffalo News sports reporter Tim Graham, who wrote the story, pointed out that Maple Leafs Sports and Entertainment, one of Bon Jovi's business partners in the Bills bid, had hired his friend Tim Leiweike as CEO to help them bring an NFL team to Toronto.[25]

Chris Pellien, of Bills Fan Thunder, was quick to pounce on Bon Jovi's PR attempt. "He's just saying what he needs to say to get his hands on our team."[26] Matthew Sabuda, president of the Buffalo Fan Alliance, an organization of loyal Bills fans, business owners and former players not connected with Bills Fan Thunder or Donald Trump, agreed with Pellien's view. "At no point in his nice letter does he say that he's not moving the team from Buffalo."[27]

Less than two weeks later, Sabuda sent the press a copy of a document he received from an anonymous emailer about Rajiv "Roger" Rai, a Rogers Communications official, one of Maple Leaf Sports and Entertainment's business partners. It said "Roger assists in the sports ownership affairs of Rogers Communications and was responsible for the acquisition of the Toronto Blue Jays and is part of the ownership group attempting to acquire and move the Buffalo Bills to Toronto."[28] The leaked document blew up in the local news media. Roger Rai denied his involvement, and he tried to explain away the document as a "mistake on my behalf"[29] but the damage was irreversible. By August 29th, Maple Leaf Sports and Entertainment had parted ways with Jon Bon Jovi,[30] but the Canadian business group couldn't match Sabres owners Terry and Kim Pegula's $1.3 billion bid to buy the Buffalo Bills. On September 9, 2014 the Bills announced that the Pegulas had reached an agreement to buy the franchise for $1.4 billion.[31]

One month later, on October 10th, the Pegulas officially took charge of the Bills. In an emotional ceremony, Terry Pegula defended his decision to spend $1.4 billion to purchase the team. "I want to ask our fans if we overpaid. I know what they will tell you. I cannot believe the pent-up fear of losing this team by our fans."[32] Pegula began his press conference by saying "My name is Terry Pegula, and the Pegulas just bought a football team. Actually, that's not totally correct. We all just bought a team, our team, the Buffalo Bills."[33]

Terry and Kim Pegula stepped in and saved the Bills from moving out of town. Donald Trump might have moved the team, or he might not have. Jon Bon Jovi and the Toronto bidding group would have certainly tried to move the Bills north. The Pegulas had saved Buffalo from going the way of St. Louis, San Diego and Oakland, all communities with loyal fan bases that lost their NFL franchises to two-faced greedy new owners and wealthier communities with more corporate sponsors, luxury boxes, ticket prices and seat licenses. But what if they hadn't? If Terry and Kim Pegula didn't intervene, how would the future of pro sports in Buffalo be different?

Jeff Miller, Bills author and historian, believes there wouldn't be a Buffalo Bills team today without the Pegula's bid. The NFL's owners would not have cared about the fans in Buffalo any more than they did for St. Louis, San Diego and Oakland fans. Greed and the almighty dollar would have carried the day. "The Pegulas buying the team was absolutely a good thing because…Bon Jovi did have it in mind to move the team. It would have been very difficult but…ultimately it would have succeeded because …if you flash enough money around the rest of the owners don't really give two cents about the city of Buffalo and the fans, they care about padding their bank accounts. But I think they would have been met with resistance from people in the league including the commissioner, (Roger Goodell) who's a Western New Yorker."[34]

Tim Graham, former Buffalo News sports reporter and senior writer at The Athletic, feels that political pressure from New York state and federal elected officials would have ensured that the Bills stayed in Buffalo, no matter who the winning bidder ultimately was. Unlike the situation in St. Louis, the NFL could not afford to cross New York politicos who would have made the league's life difficult had the NFL's owners chosen to approve a Bills franchise relocation. "Had the NFL left Buffalo, that would have drawn the ire of powerful politicians. Andrew Cuomo, of course, who some feel might be a future president of the United States. Chuck Schumer, one of the most powerful senators in the country. The NFL needed all of the political capital it could muster and still does at the time. It can't afford to go pissing off powerful politicians because they need as much help as they can get to do all the things that they want to do as a business. And the NFL is headquartered in New York City and the Buffalo Bills being the last team in New York State, I think that the NFL would have gone in the crosshairs of some very powerful politicians."[35]

Graham believes that if the Toronto group had been the winning bidder, Bon Jovi and his partners would have kept the Bills in Buffalo long-term, once they realized the NFL didn't want a franchise in Toronto. In addition, the team would have been better off under Bon Jovi's management than Pegula's, because Jon Bon Jovi did his homework and was serious about learning from successful NFL owners and coaches such as Robert Kraft and Bill Belichick of the New England Patriots. However, Donald Trump's anti-Bon Jovi media campaign sabotaged that possibility. "I think they got involved, realized that they could have bought the team. That they could buy the team and not move it was OK with them, once they realized that the NFL was not interested in the team being in Toronto."

"He (Bon Jovi) had a lot of guidance from people like Robert Kraft. He's gotten guidance over the years from Bill Belichick and he's been involved with the Arena Football League. And I think that he was taking a pretty practical approach to running a football team. He had football people around him."

"So, I think that who knows, maybe the Bills would be even farther along with Bon Jovi as the owner than it would if Terry Pegula had owned the team because

Terry Pegula came in and admitted he didn't know much about football. He let Russ Brandon continue to run football and Doug Whaley remained as the general manager and that led to the Rex Ryan hire and they're still trying to dig themselves out of that transition."

"(Trump's anti-Bon Jovi effort) was good fear mongering. And the whole Trump organization, the group, Michael Caputo, the whole thing with the campaign of Bon Jovi Free Zones did a wonderful job of making sure that the fans would not stand for Bon Jovi as the owner."[36]

Sal Maiorana, author and Rochester Democrat and Chronicle sports reporter, thinks the Toronto group would have had an uphill battle moving the Bills to Canada's largest city, mainly because Rogers Centre is not adequate for an NFL team. "Toronto… just was never going to be a viable option and the main reason was… Rogers Centre…was not going to be a viable stadium situation for the NFL. And from what I heard up there, trying to get a new stadium built was going to be a major pain in the ass. And it may not have happened, at least that's probably what would have prevented the team from going there. The NFL in no way was going to continue to play at Rogers Centre. They were OK with it for…one game a year, for that five or six years the Bills went there. But unless a new stadium was going to be built, that probably wouldn't have happened. So…I just never had a real fear that Toronto was going to be an option for the Bills. I think Bon Jovi and his group would have made it work, they probably would've pushed really hard first to begin in Buffalo (and then move) …but the Toronto situation never really concerned me much."[37]

No Toronto Bills, but possibly the L.A. Bills or the Las Vegas Bills. Matt Sabuda, Buffalo Fan Alliance president and WBFO sports commentator, feels that if the Pegulas hadn't bid on the franchise, the team would have headed to the West Coast. "Given how many other teams recently just actually moved locations, you look at how both the Rams went to L.A. and the Chargers went from San Diego also to L.A. and now the Raiders from Oakland to Las Vegas, I think unfortunately it's a real possibility that the Bills probably would be part of that carousel and… would be leaving Buffalo in two years when the lease opt-out was set to hit or in five years when the lease ended altogether. I think they…would have ended up in one of those spots where one of the other teams ended up now. I think it would have been L.A. or Vegas."[38]

Chris Ostrander, sportswriter for Two in the Box.com, is of the opinion that Buffalo dodged a bullet thanks to the Pegulas, and the Toronto group was a serious contender for any relocation effort. Bon Jovi and his partners might have run out the lease at Ralph Wilson Stadium (now Bills Stadium) the same way the Oakland to Vegas move is going now. "I have to think they're (the Bills) in Toronto, or at least on their way to Toronto. Maybe we're looking at a situation sort of like Oakland's dealing with now where you're playing out your lease, it's kind of a…dead man walking so to speak until the lease runs out, and then the team's moving on to a new location. And I know full well that there are intricacies in the lease language that would have prevented a new owner from moving the team or would have made it very difficult for them to do so at least prior to the lease's expiration."[39]

Maiorana believes the ironclad Bills lease makes it difficult for any new owner to move the team, and like Tim Graham, he was never concerned that the Bills would leave Buffalo, no matter who won the bidding war after Ralph Wilson's passing. The Bill's lease at Bills Stadium through 2022 keeps an impatient owner like Stan Kroenke from moving a team immediately, and the danger of the Bills leaving was overblown. "I always felt that the Bills real estate, even if Trump had bought them, I just had the feeling that he would keep them in Buffalo. With Bon Jovi, I don't know…I think that even if the Pegulas had not bought the team, there would have been enough provisions from Erie County, from the Bills themselves, from Ralph Wilson's estate. But I think the team would have been saved certainly through the lease at the stadium which is 2022… and then beyond, it would probably come down to could they build a new stadium. They'd own it in Buffalo. And if that were to happen, I always felt the team was going to stay put. It's great the Pegulas bought them. And I think for our sake they're probably here for generations to come. But... I always felt that they (the Bills) were going to stay put no matter who bought the team."[40]

Maiorana said that unlike in times past, there aren't many locations for new expansion teams. That makes it harder for a new owner to look elsewhere. "If you look around the country there really aren't too many places that you could move an NFL franchise to. There aren't a lot of cities that are big enough, that could provide enough of an income situation to take on an NFL team...Certainly Buffalo's a small market...They don't make a whole lot of money here but they make enough. And with the Pegula's ownership they're going to make more...But...I never really had a strong feeling that the team was in danger of leaving."[41]

Jon Bon Jovi and his partners at Maple Leaf Sports and Entertainment were one of the potential Bills bidders who tried to buy the team and failed. The other losing bidder was Donald Trump, real estate developer, reality TV show star and 45th president of the United States. Trump reportedly offered $1 billion for the franchise, but he wasn't willing to go higher and lost to Terry and Kim Pegula's $1.4 billion winning offer. If the Donald had bought the Bills, there's a good chance he wouldn't have been elected president in 2016. Buffalo News writer Tim O'Shei pointed out that "The New-York based businessman has said this many times: including to the Buffalo News. If he purchased the Buffalo Bills, he wouldn't be running for president. Think about that one."[42]

If the Pegulas hadn't bought the Bills and Trump had succeeded, how would the team fare today? The Pegulas are known for being measured, image-conscious and try to avoid negative publicity. Donald Trump would be a complete opposite as a team owner. Former NBC reporter Luke Russert told Tim O'Shei that Trump is: "Bombastic, egotistical. He would certainly have tried to shake up the owner's club as it exists. I think about who he compares to most closely. Maybe Jerry Jones? But even Jerry Jones has a point in time where he kind of falls in line and goes with the status quo. My God, imagine the quotes."[43]

Author David Cay Johnston said Trump would not have given back to the local community the way the Pegulas have. "I call him the P.T. Barnum of our age. He would have promoted the Bills, but he would not have promoted Buffalo."[44] Johnston added that Trump, like Bon Jovi and his cohorts, would have eventually moved the team, or sold it to new owners who would. "When the team went south because he had drained it of all the cash needed to make a successful franchise, or more likely he'd arranged to move it somewhere else, even as part of a sale, I think people would feel shock and betrayal. It really is fortunate for Western New York that a local person bought the team. You're not going to see the Pegulas move the team anywhere else."[45]

Tim Graham believes the NFL would have limited Donald Trump's ability to manage the Bills as he saw fit, or try to sell or move them, mainly because the NFL's owners didn't want Trump running an NFL team in the first place. "I think that Trump would have angered and irritated too many of the other owners that they would not have just allowed him to do whatever he wanted to do. Let's say he wanted to move them to St. Louis or get them to Los Angeles before the Rams could move there or be the second team in Los Angeles or Las Vegas or whatever. They (the NFL owners) didn't want him in the club to begin with. They didn't want him in their circle to begin with so let's say that there was some way that he did get in there and win the bid, that they would have allowed him to do whatever he wanted with his franchise is a stretch."[46]

Chris Ostrander thinks Trump was never a serious contender to own the Bills and that his bidding efforts weren't legitimate. "I'm of the opinion that Donald Trump's bid I don't think was ever real. I don't know what role that group was meant to play in it. I don't believe he was ever a real option to own the team. And this isn't reflective of his presidency, but just frankly his involvement in the bidding."[47]

Ostrander also said that, since Trump wasn't serious, there weren't that many people besides the Pegulas to prevent Bon Jovi and his Toronto pals from getting their hands on the Bills. Rochester billionaire Tom Golisano could have come to the rescue the way he did with the Buffalo Sabres, even though Golisano was not a major potential buyer during the sale process. "If it hadn't been for the Pegulas… we're probably talking about the team moving and sooner rather than later. It's hard to say because even if the Pegulas weren't an option…what if they weren't even the owners of the Sabres, what if they just weren't on our radar at all? Are we in a position where…someone else with deep pockets steps up? I don't think Jeffrey Gundlach is a sports guy but there are a handful of people with Buffalo ties who have pretty significant net worth. It could have been something along those lines happening, even someone like Tom Golisano doing something similar with what he did with the Sabres. Perhaps that would be a potential outcome but I would have to say the most likely …it has got to be Toronto."[48]

So, with no bid from Terry and Kim Pegula, there could be a Toronto Bills, a Los Angeles Bills or a Las Vegas Bills. Jon Bon Jovi and his partners at Maple Leaf Sports and Entertainment would have tried to move the Bills to Toronto. They might not have succeeded, if the NFL insisted on a new stadium to replace Rogers Centre, or they might have waited until the Bills' lease ran out in 2022. In addition, New York Governor Andrew Cuomo, New York Senator Charles Schumer and NFL Commissioner and Jamestown, NY native Roger Goodell could have intervened. Donald Trump might still be a private citizen if he bought the team, running shows like The Apprentice while Hillary Clinton ran the White House. Possibly Trump would wait until the Bills' lease expired, then sell the team to out-of-town investors like Maple Leaf Sports and Entertainment, who bid their time to get a hold of a lucrative NFL franchise. Maybe Tom Golisano owns the Bills and has them play one game a year in Rochester instead of Rogers Centre. One thing is for sure, with Terry and Kim Pegula in charge, the Bills are staying in Western New York for a long time to come.

Ostrander stressed that nobody in Buffalo should minimize how lucky Bills fans are for the Pegula purchase, an intervention that was nothing short of miraculous. "I remember …that the Pegulas were asked if they were even interested in buying the Bills and if I'm not mistaken…their answers always came back to, no we're happy with the Sabres. We're not looking to purchase another team or expand our portfolio further…There are a lot of moving pieces there…I guess it's kind of fascinating to think that Terry Pegula came along. First, before the Sabres even to give so much money to Penn State and their hockey program and then the Sabres purchase follows fairly quickly thereafter and then all of a sudden it just really becomes something of a white knight for the region. It all happened in quick succession. It's kind of amazing to think about the timeline."[49]

A sellout crowd fills Ralph Wilson Stadium (now Bills Stadium) for a Buffalo Bills game just days after the Pegulas finalized ownership of the team, Oct. 12, 2014. Without owners committed to keeping the Bills in Buffalo, the franchise might have moved to Toronto, Los Angeles or Las Vegas. *Photo by P.A. Fraterrigo. Licensed under the Creative Commons, https://creativecommons.org/licenses/by/2.0/*

CHAPTER 2
What if the Buffalo Bills Won Super Bowl XXV?

THE BUFFALO BILLS WERE riding high at the end of the 1990-91 season. They had gone to the playoffs with a 13-3 winning record, and the Bills' playoff victories only cemented their air of inevitability. As well as finishing the season with 13 wins and only 3 losses, the Bills had "Squished the Fish" by knocking out rival quarterback Dan Marino and the Miami Dolphins with a 44-34 playoff win. Then Buffalo went on to completely annihilate the L.A. Raiders 51-3, the most one-sided trounce in AFC Championship history.

Buffalo Bills quarterback Jim Kelly looks for an open receiver as L.A. Raiders defensive end Howie Long tries to tackle him during the first quarter of the AFC Championship Game, Jan. 20, 1991. The Bills would win the game 51-3, one of the most one-sided victories in AFC Championship history. *Photo by AP.*

The Bills had also defeated the Giants in the regular season when they met at Giants Stadium, 17-13.[1] Bills quarterback Jim Kelly said "I don't know if we ever clicked better offensively than we did in those two games. Just about everything we tried worked. We were in a zone."[2] The Bills had the NFL's best offense in the 1990 season,[3] they'd racked up 95 points in their first two playoff games,[4] and it seemed like no team could stop them from winning the Lombardi Trophy.

The bookies in Vegas had declared the Bills the favorite.[5] L.A. Times Staff Writer Bob Oates wrote that "The Bills are favored over the Giants. Many observers say that the NFC's Giants were honed in a tougher league. But most football fans, remembering Buffalo's 51-3 victory over the Raiders, are sticking with the Bills."[6]

Football fans weren't the only ones impressed by the Bills' 51-3 thrashing. New York Giants tight end Mark Bavaro was intimidated. He later told New York Daily News sportswriter Hank Gola that he wasn't confident the Giants would win the Super Bowl because the Bills were a high-scoring team and the Giants weren't. Going into the game, Bavaro didn't see how the Giants could match the Bills point for point.[7]

Giants linebacker Carl Banks felt that it was a season where no one really expected New York to be a serious contender. Each week the Giants won seemed like a fluke. When he and his teammates heard about the Bill's AFC championship victory and saw the game film they were seriously impressed and felt way over-matched.[8] Giants center Bart Oates thought looking back on Super Bowl XXV that if New York played the game 10 times, they might have won two or three.[9] Even Giants coach Bill Parcells didn't sound sure his team could pull off an upset. "I think our team is prepared to play and I think we'll play hard. It doesn't mean we're going to win, but we'll give it our best shot."[10]

Giants defensive coordinator Bill Belichick normally followed a time-honored philosophy of "stop the run."[11] Belichick had always believed in limiting the yards that running backs would pick up. However, he told a room full of disbelieving Giants players six days before Super Bowl XXV that they were going to let Bills running back Thurman Thomas get 100 yards.[12] The atmosphere became hostile, and the guys in the locker room told Belichick that his plan was insulting. Carl Banks remembered that they didn't want anybody to get that many yards. However, as Belichick began to explain his idea, the players warmed up to his strategy. The defensive coordinator planned to limit the time the Bills' offense was on the field, and when the Bills did have the ball, he wanted the Giants defense to keep quarterback Jim Kelly from completing too many passes to his wide receivers, while letting Thurman Thomas get as many yards as he wished.

At the start of the game, the Bills had the ball first, but the Giants forced them to punt on their opening drive. Once the Giants got possession, they took 6:15 off the clock, marched 58 yards down the field, and set up kicker Matt Bahr with a 28-yard field goal. The Bills answered back with a 66-yard drive. Jim Kelly threw a 61-yard completion to wide receiver James Lofton that set kicker Scott Norwood up with a 23-yard field goal to tie the game, 3-3.[13] The Bills forced the Giants to punt on their possession, then Kelly and his K-Gun no huddle offense went to work, going on a 12 play 80-yard drive that worked so well the Bills never had a third down. Buffalo scored a touchdown early in the second quarter to make the score 10-3.[14]

The Bills pinned the Giants at their own 7-yard line. Bills defensive end Bruce Smith sacked Giants quarterback Jeff Hostetler in the end zone for a two-point safety. Smith tried to force Hostetler to fumble the ball and make it a seven-point gain, but the Giants quarterback held the ball away from him so the Bills only picked up a safety.[15] Then the Giants went 87 yards to score a touchdown with 25 seconds left in the half to cut their deficit to just two points.

At the beginning of the 3rd Quarter, the score was Bills 12, Giants 10. The Giants made another long 75-yard drive and scored on Otis Anderson's 1-yard touchdown run to take a 17-12 lead. New York's power defense forced the Bills to punt again, then drove to Buffalo's 35-yard line. At 4th down and 2, Bruce Smith tackled Anderson and Buffalo took over. They moved the ball 63 yards in four plays. Then Thurman Thomas ran 31 yards on the 1st play of the 4th quarter to give the Bills a 19-17 lead.[16]

Bill Parcell's team made another long and clock-consuming drive that took 7:32 and gave the Giants a 20-19 lead with another Bahr field goal. The Giants and Bills took turns making each other punt, then Buffalo finally got the ball back at their own 10-yard line late in 4th quarter with 2:16 left to play.[17] Thurman Thomas made a critical seven yard run to get the Bills to the Giants' 29-yard line with eight seconds to go. Scott Norwood kicked a 47-yard field goal attempt that sailed wide right and missed the goal post by three feet.[18] The Giants ran out the clock, and the Bills left the field without a Super Bowl win.

Buffalo Bills kicker Scott Norwood kicks the field goal that misses on the last play of Super Bowl XXV, Jan. 27, 1991. If Norwood had succeeded, the Bills would have won the Super Bowl. *Photo by AP.*

Super Bowl XXV should have been a Bills victory. The Giants barely won, 20-19, but one point was all they needed. Monday morning quarterbacking is a time-honored ritual among defeated players and fans after any game, not to mention the Super Bowl. Bills fans in Western New York lamented the defeat for years, and it was compounded by further losses in Super Bowls XXVI, XXVII and XX-VIII.

Bills linebacker Darryl Talley believed Scott Norwood shouldn't take the blame for losing the Super Bowl. If the rest of the team had played better throughout the game, the Bills might have won it. "That was the most visible play of the game, but it was all those invisible plays that caused us to lose"[19] he told author Scott Pitoniak. "Missed tackles. Missed blocks. Dropped passes. Overthrown balls. Blown coverages. People still want to pin it all on Scottie, and that's bull. We all made contributions to that loss. I know I made my share of mistakes, and I told Scottie that afterward."[20]

Bills starting linebacker Ray Bentley thought the Giants had a better coaching strategy. "We were outcoached. I don't mean that in a derogatory way against Marv Levy and our staff, but rather as a compliment to Bill Parcells. There was only one way for them to beat us, and that was by keeping our offense on the sidelines. That's exactly what they did."[21] Indeed, the Giants held the ball for the majority of Super Bowl XXV and kept the Bills' fast moving K-Gun offense off the field for more than 40 minutes.

If Bill Belichick had stayed with his original philosophy of stop the run, Buffalo's offense might have marched up the field repeatedly, with Jim Kelly throwing long passes to wide receivers Andre Reed and James Lofton with ease. Instead, the Giants let Thurman Thomas run the ball and hammered the receivers, and the Bills failed to score a single touchdown pass.

Another factor that contributed to the Giants' win was Bills players celebrating all week as if they'd already won the Super Bowl. Bills coach Marv Levy didn't reign in his crew, and the high-riding AFC champions lived it up at Tampa's watering holes. Buffalo News sports columnist Vic Carucci pointed out that the Bills were partying when they should have been practicing. Levy didn't give them a curfew early in the week, and they took full advantage of that fact. More than one player told Carucci they regretted treating the Super Bowl like a spring break party instead of a business trip.[22]

If Bills coach Marv Levy had remembered the discipline of his days in the Army

Air Force during World War II and clamped down on his team's late night fun, a more rested, focused Bills offensive line could have worn down the New York Giants and gained more yards and points. If the Bills had managed to play better at the game and party after the Super Bowl, Belichick had kept to his original game plan of stopping the run, Bruce Smith had made Hostetler fumble in the Giants end zone, or Norwood had somehow made that kick, how would things be different in the sports universe? One change that alters the football landscape would be, possibly no Bills team making four straight Super Bowl appearances. The feat that hasn't happened before or since may not have happened at all had Buffalo won the Lombardi Trophy on January 27, 1991.

Jeff Miller, Bills author and historian, believes "it's very possible that if they had won Super Bowl XXV, they would not have gone back to the other three. I think that that resiliency to prove that they were worthy, is what kept them going back every time they lost. It's like 'no we've got to get back in and prove ourselves.' So, if they had won the first one, they probably would have been more content to maybe not play as well as they did. They were a resilient group of people but they also had their weaknesses. They had some arrogance about them and I truly believe that that was part of the problem in Super Bowl XXV."

"Many of them admitted they were out partying during the week. So, you can extrapolate from that and say well, okay, that's how they were leading up to the game. They won. They would have said, 'well gee we partied and we still won, that's how good we are.' Who knows if the wheels would have blown up after that, but I think it's very likely…that if they had won that game they would not have gone to four. Maybe they would have bounced back and … gone to (Super Bowl) XXVII or XXVIII but four in a row? I doubt it and I don't think you're ever going to see any team ever go to four in a row again."[23]

Sal Maiorana, author and Rochester Democrat and Chronicle sports reporter, agrees. "If they had won Super Bowl XXV they would have remained highly competitive. I don't know that they would have gone back to four in a row. Maybe…

the year after they might have gone back. Because that was actually the best team. The' 91 team was the more talented team. Statistically it was their most dominant year on offense. And the AFC really wasn't that strong (in those years). The Bills made it four years in a row. It wasn't an overpowering conference by any means."

"So, there might have been a chance they could have kept going back. But my sense has always been if they'd won the first one, they might have gone back for the second one and that might have been it...That was a team that was filled with guys who enjoyed their good time. They had fun and I wonder what that type of success winning the Super Bowl would have done to those guys. Maybe it would have gone to their heads a little bit. I think (they kept going back) because they lost, and kept losing. They were a very determined bunch...They were the kings of perseverance and that's what pushed them back each year, the fact that they did lose in the Super Bowl. But...if they had won the first one, I really don't think that they would have had four straight appearances in the Super Bowl."[24]

Matt Sabuda, WBFO sports commentator, like Jeff Miller and Sal Maiorana, thinks a Bills' Super Bowl win in XXV, as hard as it was to beat the Giants, would make it easier for the Bills to rest on their NFL laurels. "People say that if they'd won the first one, there would have been a chance for them to win others. I'm not sure that necessarily correlates. For instance, people say that, well (had) they got that one under their belt, they would have been a more formidable team going forward. I think if they...won the first one there's a pretty significant chance they would not have gone back to the three additional...Either they would have just been in the mix, they might have gone back to one or two but I sincerely doubt they would have done the four Super Bowls in a row like they did. That team, from everything I recall...had a bit of a reputation for being big partiers, and...had they got that one Super Bowl under their belt, it would have been too easy to see some of those guys really let it go to their head quickly and lose some of that hunger to go back."[25]

Chris Ostrander, sportswriter for Two in the Box.com, believes Super Bowl

XXV wasn't Buffalo's only best chance, and the team might have had an equally good opportunity to win Super Bowl XXVIII. "I often wonder if XXVIII wasn't their 'best shot.' They led at halftime, it seemed as if they had things figured out a little bit more that year and then Thurman fumbled, the defense simply couldn't keep up with the second half, and they ended up getting beat 30-13 in the final. But I often think about XXVIII even more than XXV because maybe there are more alternatives, XXV is just if he makes the kick they win it right? So maybe that's why I think of XXVIII a little bit more."[26]

Ostrander said it was difficult for any AFC team to win during the early '90s, because the NFC was so dominant during that decade. "The other thing I always think about is just how good the NFC was during that stretch...That fell right in the middle of 10-15 straight Super Bowl victories for the NFC. I don't think it got broken until Denver had done it until '97... The NFC had won...a good number of Super Bowls in a row and...just those two Dallas teams produced so good. The Bills were a little unlucky... just who they ran into and when...Obviously, we'd all breathe a little easier had they won one of them, and...everyone would have traded the other three appearances for one win."[27]

Tim Graham, former Buffalo News sports reporter and senior writer at The Athletic, believes the Jim Kelly Era Bills gained more respect in hindsight by going to four Super Bowls in a row rather than winning one, even though the majority of Bills fans might prefer a single Lombardi Trophy. "All the people who were great on those teams all got into the Hall of Fame. They are all legends. Jim Kelly would still be Jim Kelly. I don't think it really would change much in terms of individuals and how we view them. Especially as time has gone on...going to four straight Super Bowls has gained more respect than winning one. I've heard that discussion of, what would you rather do? Go to four straight Super Bowls or win one? Maybe the fans would pick win one. But anybody who reflects back with any deep thought, what's harder to do? It's harder to go to four straight Super Bowls than it is just to win the one."[28]

What else would change? Some say a Bills Super Bowl victory in Tampa might have doomed Bill Belichick's prospects, the man that sports media pundits praised as "brilliant", "original" and a "genius"[29] for pulling off the Giants upset. If the Giants had lost that game, nobody would have considered the legendarily poker-faced, surly and arrogant defensive coordinator as any of those things. Bill Belichick needed a win to advance his career, and without Super Bowl XXV, he would have remained a defensive coordinator or an assistant.

Even after that win, Belichick had a stormy eight years of coaching jobs, first head coach in Cleveland, Browns owner Art Modell firing him, then working under Bill Parcells for the Patriots, then following Parcells to the Jets, then head coach of the Jets for one day before quitting. Parcells' and Belichick's rocky relationship came to a head one day. During a game working under Parcells, Belichick called a blitz. Parcells didn't want to blitz, but he let his defensive coordinator call the play. The blitz worked, and Parcells, irritated at being proven wrong, growled sarcastically over his microphone "Yeah, you're a genius, everybody knows it, a goddamn genius, but that's why you failed as a head coach-that's why you'll never be a head coach."[30] Without his win over the Bills, Belichick might never have been a head coach in the first place.

Patriots owner Bob Kraft finally landed Belichick as head coach in 2000. Less than two years later, Patriots quarterback Drew Bledsoe became injured in the second week of the season. Belichick decided to put in a little-known second-string quarterback named Tom Brady. The coach didn't make Brady starting quarterback until Week Eleven, but when he did, Brady helped the Pats win their last six regular season games, and then, a Super Bowl.[31] The Belichick-Brady partnership that dominated the NFL's AFC East Division for almost 20 years and filled Bills supporters and the rest of football fandom outside New England with loathing might never have come to pass.

Tim Graham believes a Bills Super Bowl XXV win would have given Buffalo a powerful psychological shot in the arm, even if Western New York's economy and

Buffalo's downtown redevelopment would not have happened any faster. The Bills would still be Super Bowl champions, and that fact would have quieted Buffalo bashers from the early '90s to the present day. "Had Scott Norwood's kick gone through the uprights I think that Buffalo would always have that retort. They're on the list. They've got the ring, they can hang a Lombardi Trophy in the field house. They can have it out at the stadium. There's a banner, there's some power in that. They can say they were champions at one time as opposed to being on that short list with four or five teams that haven't won one."

"I don't know that it would change the city. I don't think that it would have helped the Buffalo Renaissance happen any faster. I think that it would have remained a Rust Belt town. The plants would remain closed or continued to close. I don't think that you'd have Canalside any sooner or HarborCenter any sooner."[32]

No Giants victory in Super Bowl XXV, and no Bill Belichick playbook in the Pro Football Hall of Fame. Buffalo's famous inferiority complex would have taken a serious dent, decades before Canalside, downtown loft conversions, One Buffalo and Pegulaville. Western New Yorkers on cross country flights and out-of-town conventions could shove the Super Bowl win in outsider's faces when they sneered at Buffalo and made cracks about the region's weather throughout the 1990s and beyond. Perhaps with no Dallas Cowboys 52-17 victory over the Bills in 1993, Jimmy Johnson wouldn't be a regular commentator on Fox NFL Sunday.

When the defeated Super Bowl XXV Bills team got off the plane from Tampa, a crowd of 25,000 fans had braved icy winds and freezing temperatures to fill Niagara Square in downtown Buffalo to give the players gracious condolences. Bills supporters held signs saying "USA! "and "Thank You Bills!".[33] Right before the official program started, the crowd started chanting "We want Scott! We want Scott!"[34] Kicker Scott Norwood made his way to the microphone, and was touched by the outpouring of support. He told the cheering fans that he never felt more loved than right then.[35]

Imagine if the Bills had won that Super Bowl, and delirious, ecstatic Bills supporters had descended on local bars and restaurants, partying the way only Buffalo's hard-working, hard-living, hard-drinking citizens can.

On August 28, 2018, a new play debuted at Shea's Smith Theatre in Buffalo. Titled "ONCE IN MY LIFETIME: A Buffalo Football Fantasy" the play explores what would happen if the Bills won a Super Bowl.[36] With local owners committed to keeping the team in Buffalo, and the Bills ending a 17-year playoff drought at the end of the 2017-18 season, fans will have plenty of chances in the years to come to see if this long-awaited outcome will finally happen.

CHAPTER 3
What if the Buffalo Bills Hadn't Selected Jim Kelly in the 1983 NFL Draft?

In THE EARLY 1980s, THE Buffalo Bills needed a boost. The Bills had ended the shortened 1982 season with a 4-5 record and missed the playoffs. Since trading running back O.J. Simpson to the San Francisco 49ers in 1977,[1] the franchise had struggled to draft new players who could excite the city's fan base.

Bills staff and coaches checked into New York's Sheraton Hotel in late April 1983, where the NFL held its annual draft on April 26-27.[2] The draft was unusual from the start, with six quarterbacks available in the first round. What was stranger was what happened when the Baltimore Colts selected the first pick of the draft, quarterback John Elway. Elway refused to sign with Baltimore. At the time, New York Yankees owner George Steinbrenner was aggressively courting Elway to join the Yankees as a baseball player. Elway and his agent successfully used the threat of the quarterback leaving football to persuade the Colts to trade him to the Denver Broncos six days after the draft.[3]

John Elway wasn't the only young prospect who balked at going where he was drafted. Jim Kelly was an up-and-coming young quarterback from the University of Miami. Kelly had a taste of palm trees and tropical weather, and the Pennsylvania native didn't want to play for any team located in a cold climate. Kelly recalled "My agent looked at me after Elway got picked and the problem that arose from it and he said, 'Hey Jim, is there anywhere you don't want to play? I said, 'Oh yeah, I don't want to play for the Minnesota Vikings, I don't want to play for the Green Bay Packers and I don't want to play for the Buffalo Bills."[4] Kelly was eligible to be the 12th pick of the first round. When the Buffalo Bills selected Notre Dame tight end Tony Hunter, Jim Kelly began celebrating. "I remember jumping out of my seat and I hit my mother who was sitting on the right arm of the recliner and I knocked her right off the chair. I felt so bad, I quick picked her up off the floor and I'm apologizing, 'Sorry, Mom, I'm just glad I'm not going to play for Buffalo.'"[5]

Kelly wasn't in the clear yet, however. The Bills also had the 14th pick, and they chose Jim Kelly. The young quarterback was stunned. "I couldn't believe it. Within minutes the phone calls came and with me being politically correct I was saying how excited I was to be a Buffalo Bill. And when I hung up I said, 'We need to call the USFL and see what other options we have.'"[6] The United States Football League was founded in 1982 to play football in the spring and summer during the NFL's offseason. The league didn't compete directly with the NFL for games, but did compete for football talent. One of those USFL franchises, the Houston Gamblers, had their eye on Kelly. While Kelly and his agent, Greg Lustig were in the Bill's office getting ready to sign a contract with the Bills, Houston Gamblers owner Dr. Jerry Argovitz called the office and asked for Lustig. He told the secretary that he was the agent's brother-in-law and that Lustig had a family emergency. That got Lustig on the phone. Once Argovitz had Lustig on the line, he convinced the agent to fly Kelly down to Houston and sign him with the Gamblers for a $3.5 million contract.[7]

The Bills were stunned. Bills GM Paul McGroder told the press the Bills considered three different offers that Kelly and his agent made and they were very happy with the offer the Bills made to them. McGroder added that it wasn't the Buffalo Bills who let the fans down.[8] Greg Lustig trashed-talked Buffalo in front of the Houston media, telling them it was one of the most depressed areas in America and that (Bills running back) Joe Cribbs made under $500 in personal appearances there during the last three years.[9]

Kelly played for three seasons with the Houston Gamblers, and he threw for 9,842 yards and 83 touchdowns. In 1984, he became the USFL MVP, and set a league record of 5,219 passing yards and 44 touchdown passes.[10] Jim Kelly was playing well for the Gamblers, but all of owner Jerry Argovitz's Texas swagger couldn't help the United States Football League compete against the established NFL.

Another league owner with New York braggadocio, real estate mogul Donald Trump, had pushed the USFL to move its schedule from spring and summer to fall. Trump sounded theological when he said "If God wanted football in the spring, He wouldn't have created baseball."[11] After the league's third season, Trump persuaded the other owners to move to a fall schedule. Dr. Ted Dietrich, Chicago Blitz owner, disagreed with the decision. Dietrich thought it was a big mistake and he was concerned that trying to compete with the NFL would end in disaster.[12]

Trump not only convinced the USFL to switch to a fall schedule, he also engineered a merger between his New Jersey Generals and Argovitz's Houston Gamblers after the 1985 season. Trump called it a "dream team" that would have Jim Kelly as quarterback, Herschel Walker as running back and Ricky Sanders as receiver. The Generals' owner thought it was the best team in football.[13] Kelly was excited to be on board. "What I'd really like to do is play for the New Jersey Generals and Donald Trump and merge with the NFL and take the run-and-shoot with Herschel Walker in the backfield and just kick ass."[14]

Dr. Dietrich's misgivings about the USFL's new fall lineup proved to be right. The league couldn't land the TV contracts that NFL teams enjoyed, and several franchises were having financial troubles. The USFL's owners decided to sue the NFL with an anti-trust lawsuit.[15] Trump felt confident the USFL would win the suit and win handsomely. "If we win, we will have more money than the NFL, and that will be interesting"[16] he told Sports Illustrated. "We already have teams that would beat most NFL teams."[17] Trump was right about the outcome, but not about the settlement. The courts agreed that the NFL violated anti-trust laws, but only awarded the USFL $3.[18] The upstart league was finished.

Meanwhile, the Bills limped along with a string of lackluster quarterbacks including Joe Ferguson, Joe Dufek, Bruce Mathison and Vince Ferragamo. The team finished both the 1984 and 1985 seasons at 2-14. Attendance at Rich Stadium during 1985 fell to an average of 30,000 fans per game. Things got so bad that Bills owner Ralph Wilson considered an offer from Philadelphia Eagles owner Leonard Tose to trade the Bills for the Eagles.[19]

Even when the USFL was falling apart, Jim Kelly still didn't want to sign with the Bills, who had options on him. He told reporters he wouldn't go to Buffalo. "I'll never play there" he declared.[20] Kelly threatened to sit out the 1986 season so he could become an NFL free agent. The quarterback could do it, because he'd signed a personal services contract with owner Donald Trump that paid him $800,000 if he didn't play.[21] Kelly thought his career would take a dive if he went to Buffalo. "I was doing my best to make sure it wouldn't work out between me and the Bills"[22] he recalled. "I wanted them to trade me to a team like the Oakland Raiders or the Pittsburgh Steelers. I wanted to go someplace where I would have a chance to win, and to be honest, I didn't think the Bills were committed to winning."[23]

Several NFL teams, including the L.A. Raiders, contacted the Bills to see if they could acquire his rights. Bills GM Bill Polian considered it, and told his boss, team owner Ralph Wilson. "You had to listen because Jim seemed serious about not coming here. I told Wilson about the offers, and he said no. Give Mr. Wilson credit. Refusing to trade the rights to Jim has to go down as one of the greatest decisions in franchise history."[24]

Kelly had bolted for the Houston Gamblers in 1983, and Wilson didn't want him to get away a second time. "I knew we were never going to turn things around if we didn't resolve the quarterback problem"[25] Wilson remembered. "Everything we had seen and heard about Kelly indicated that he was the talented and brash quarterback we needed."[26]

Jim Kelly didn't want to come to the Queen City, but he was later grateful that Wilson didn't sell his rights. "It's funny how things turn out sometimes"[27] he told author Scott Pitoniak. "Looking back, I'm so happy Ralph Wilson didn't listen to me and trade me before I came to Buffalo, because who knows what would have happened."[28]

With the USFL defunct and Ralph Wilson refusing to sell his rights, Jim Kelly and his agents sat down with Bills management and worked out a deal. Two weeks before the 1986 season started, the Bills agreed to pay Kelly $8.5 million over five years, and Kelly took the offer. As soon as he got to Buffalo, the new quarterback got the red-carpet treatment. A police motorcade escorted him along with Ralph Wilson to a news conference in downtown Buffalo, past cheering crowds who lined the 33 expressway. New York Governor Mario Cuomo called Kelly to congratulate him. Within two weeks, the Bills had sold 10,000 season tickets.[29]

Buffalo Bills quarterback Jim Kelly holds up his new jersey with team owner Ralph Wilson in 1986. The Bills had initially drafted Kelly in 1983, but he refused to play in Buffalo and signed with the Houston Gamblers of the USFL. When the USFL folded, Kelly agreed to join the Bills and became one of the best QBs in franchise history. Kelly wore the same number, 12, with both the Gamblers and the Bills. *Photo © USA TODAY NETWORK*

The Buffalo Bills didn't turn around immediately, but GM Bill Polian picked a talented supporting cast of players to help his new quarterback win. Starting in 1988, the Bills led the AFC East with four consecutive playoff appearances. They would go on to make eight, and of course four times in the Super Bowl. In any statistic, yards per game, touchdowns, passes, runs, completions, wins, Jim Kelly is probably the greatest quarterback the Bills ever had, and the early '90s, the Jim Kelly Era, is the Bills' golden age, a time that hasn't been equaled before or since. The irony is that it all came so close to not happening. If Kelly refused to sign with Buffalo after the USFL folded, Ralph Wilson had sold his rights or Donald Trump hadn't persuaded the USFL owners to switch to a fall schedule or pursue a disastrous anti-trust lawsuit, how would the future of Bills football have turned out?

Jeff Miller, author and Bills historian, thinks the Bills would have remained a mediocre team without Jim Kelly. He helped change Buffalo's losing culture, and attract other talented players who wanted to win. "They never would have gotten anywhere (without Kelly). You've got to remember who was quarterbacking the team at the time, Bruce Mathison? Joe Dufek? These guys? Come on! They could have had Frank Reich, but even Frank Reich was not a proven starter. Jim Kelly was the touchstone. He was a guy who took the team from what they were and made them into something. Yeah, they had Andre Reed, they had Bruce Smith, they had Darryl Talley and a few others, but once they got Jim Kelly, other people really wanted to start playing for Buffalo. I think it starts with that and without him they would have been just another fair to middling team throughout the '80s."[30]

Sal Maiorana, author and Rochester Democrat and Chronicle sports reporter, believes that without Jim Kelly, Ralph Wilson might have sold the team decades before Terry and Kim Pegula ever bid on the Bills. "I really think that if the USFL hadn't folded, and the Bills hadn't been able to get Kelly, there was a good chance… that Ralph Wilson might have moved the franchise. Because he had barked about it for a long time that he would move the team if the fans didn't start coming out and they were getting…25,000 for some of those games. In the late '84-'85 season the Bills were really in a bad way. Bruce Smith and Andre Reed had come in '85, but Kelly really was the key moment for the franchise in '86."

"I didn't have that fear right before the Pegulas bought the team but I had the fear back then that Ralph was going to move the team. He had more options back then, the NFL hadn't expanded…for instance Houston was on the table, a couple of other places, too. So, there was a chance back then that they could have moved them, but getting Kelly…solidified the franchise in Buffalo. It gave the team hope, it gave the fans hope and… with Bill Polian in charge, they were able to get enough of the other team around Kelly that they built back up and they sustained it…Kelly was pretty much the central piece of the puzzle as far as I'm concerned."[31]

Maiorana feels that Kelly came in at the right moment, because the Bills desperately needed a quarterback to turn the team around. If Wilson and Polian hadn't signed him, the Bills wouldn't have made it. "That would have been a death blow to the franchise because at that time they had no real quarterback. They hadn't had a quarterback since Joe Ferguson left. He actually played in '84 but he wasn't very good, his last decent year was '83, then declined. So, they had nobody in the pipeline that could have taken over. As we saw in '84, '85 they were horrible. They were a horrible team (overall) and they were horrible at quarterback, too."[32]

Matt Sabuda, WBFO sports commentator, is of the opinion that if the Bills hadn't selected Jim Kelly in the 1983 draft, quarterback Dan Marino was also available. It's interesting to ponder what might have been if the Bills had drafted Marino. "The way the story goes…is that the Bills would have been comfortable selecting Dan Marino if they didn't take Jim Kelly so that would have been interesting to see how that played out. If Dan Marino actually ended up in Buffalo… as much as Jim Kelly was successful here, he (Marino) might have been a better fit instantly because of the likelihood of him going to the USFL was next to nothing. He went to the Dolphins and made it to a Super Bowl in his rookie year. He was coming from the University of Pittsburgh. He was not at all unwilling to be in a cold weather city like Kelly was after spending all that time at the University of

Miami. So just a little part of me wonders what would have happened if Marino would have stepped into the Bills in 1983, got some additional seasoning under his belt and had a chance to play with Thurman Thomas and a defense represented by Bruce Smith. Because he had never had that before he got to Miami."[33]

Tim Graham, former Buffalo News sports reporter and senior writer at The Athletic, agrees with Sabuda that Dan Marino was the most likely Bills quarterback without a Kelly pick. However, Marino may have gone to the USFL, just like Jim Kelly did, because Buffalo had a terrible reputation at the time. "My guess is Buffalo was such a train wreck at the time, the guys didn't want to play there he probably would've gone to the USFL, too. But the USFL would have folded just the same and he would have ended up coming back to the Bills at some point. Let's say the Bills draft him at No. 12. He says no thanks I'm going to go sign with the Pittsburgh Maulers. Pittsburgh had a team in the USFL so let's say he goes and plays for his hometown team, the Pittsburgh Maulers. The Bills still hold his rights just like they still held Jim Kelly's rights. So, when the USFL folded Dan Marino would have had nowhere else to go but the Buffalo Bills. Which was what happened with Jim Kelly, he was handcuffed, he had no other options. So, I would say it would have maybe run a parallel line. Because you're talking about two of the all-time great quarterbacks."[34]

Graham added that Dan Marino may have regretted going to Miami instead of Buffalo in the long run, because he could have gone to four Super Bowls instead of one. He would have had some great players to work with. "They would have had somebody like Thurman Thomas. It's fun to think about. He would have been throwing to some great receivers like…Andre Reed and James Lofton. I would like to think that maybe Dan Marino wishes the tables had been turned. He would have gone to more than just the one Super Bowl his rookie year. Maybe he would have been the one to go to four straight and win a couple."[35]

Chris Ostrander, sportswriter for Two in the Box.com, believes it was a good thing for Jim Kelly to go to the USFL for a few years and develop as a player before signing with the Bills. Playing quarterback for the Houston Gamblers gave Kelly time to mature away from the glare of the media spotlight. "I actually think Kelly, and more so the Bills probably benefited from his decision to go to the USFL. I almost feel like he was able to develop as a quarterback a little bit without the additional pressure that he might have faced stepping right into an NFL team. Different world obviously in the early and mid '80s than we're in today when it comes to the way players are evaluated, the pressure that they face."

Houston Gamblers quarterback Jim Kelly looks for an open receiver as Denver Gold defensive end Bruce Thornton closes in during the first quarter at the Houston Astrodome, March 18, 1985. Some sports observers believe Kelly benefitted from his USFL stint, because he joined the Bills as a proven QB instead of an untested rookie. *Photo by AP.*

"I do think that there probably would have been a little bit of a difference. You would have been walking into a different locker room and a different set of expectations for sure. If he had gone somewhere else and... become a free agent signed elsewhere, I'd be curious to know where he winds up... I think he still would have been a very good quarterback. I don't think he would have made four Super Bowl appearances, probably not. The fact is that he did end up in a good situation...in Buffalo, with a very impressive talent in terms of Reed, Thurman, James Lofton, once he came along. They had some very impressive weapons for him to work with. We had a very good line as well. So, he did step into a good situation...I would say if nothing else even as iconic as a player as he is for the Bills, he would have been for wherever else he played for."[36]

Tim Graham agrees with Ostrander that Jim Kelly's initial refusal to play for the Bills was a blessing in disguise, because Kelly developed the confidence to become a football superstar in an upstart league. He rode into Buffalo as a conquering hero, instead of an untested rookie, thanks to his stint in the USFL. The USFL was also a testing ground for many of the Bills' other talents, including their coach and GM. "So, if Jim Kelly comes straight to the Bills what happens? Well, maybe he loses his swagger, maybe he gets some of that confidence knocked out of him with the Bills. What he was able to do with the Houston Gamblers made him who he was, I think between the years in terms of the confidence, the ego. Larger than life. He knew that he was great. Had he gone straight to the Buffalo Bills, I'm sure he would have struggled. He even struggled when he came to the Bills after a few years in the USFL. I mean it wasn't like he was a superstar right out of the shoe. He had his moments where he showed that he still needed to grow to be an NFL quarterback."

"So, I think that the USFL, him going there probably worked out well for the Bills. They got a more polished product by the time he arrived. The Bills were able to get so many other people from the USFL like Kent Hull, Marv Levy their coach, Bill Polian their general manager. The USFL served the Bills. So that was a good thing. Scott Norwood came from the USFL."[37]

Without Jim Kelly, there might not be a NFL franchise in Buffalo today. Or maybe Dan Marino would have taken the Bills to Super Bowl glory. Possibly if Kelly signed with the Bills in 1983 instead of 1986, he would have languished as a second-string quarterback behind Joe Ferguson. Certainly, the Bills would not have made four straight Super Bowl appearances between 1991 and 1994, and the golden era of the early '90s Bills would not exist. One thing is for sure, Bills fans are lucky that Jim Kelly came along and eventually agreed to be Buffalo's quarterback for 10 years. He helped turn a struggling team around, and gave a down on its luck city and region a much-needed sports shot in the arm. He led his team to the Super Bowl four times, and even though they didn't win it, Kelly and his crew gave Buffalo some of the best football seasons it's ever had. For that, Bills fans will always be grateful.

CHAPTER 4
What if Ralph Wilson Had Been Able to
Buy an AFL Franchise in Miami instead of Buffalo?

In the 1950s, football was a growing sport in the United States. Long a
standard feature on college campuses, the game was becoming a more popular
pastime for audiences of all ages. The National Football League had dominated the
game since the 1920s and had successfully fought off any rival leagues that tried
to challenge its monopoly. NFL attendance had grown from nearly 2 million in
1950 to more than 3 million in 1958.[1] In 1956, Chicago Bears owner George Halas
predicted the NFL would expand from 12 to 16 teams sometime in the 1960s.
Two years later, NFL Commissioner Bert Bell appointed George Halas and Pittsburgh Steelers owner Art Rooney to a committee to explore expansion teams. The
committee identified five cities that they thought could support an NFL franchise:
Dallas and Houston, Texas, Minneapolis-St. Paul Minnesota, Buffalo, New York
and Miami, Florida.[2]

That same year, two Texas businessmen, Lamar Hunt and Bud Adams, applied
to the NFL for expansion teams in Dallas and Houston. However, the league ownership said no. The two tycoons then tried to buy the Chicago Cardinals and move
them to Texas and the NFL rebuffed them again. Halas and Rooney scheduled an
NFL preseason game in Houston in 1959. Halas thought the league would start expanding in 1960 with teams in Dallas, Houston, Buffalo and Miami being the most
likely. When the NFL tried to use Rice University's field for a Houston expansion
team the school refused. At that point, the league's power brokers lost interest in
Houston and began to look at Minneapolis instead.[3] Lamar Hunt lost his patience

with the NFL, and he hit on the idea of starting a rival league to bring professional football to cities the NFL was too slow to consider. The American Football League was born, with its first organizational meeting in Chicago in mid-August 1959.[4]

Hunt wanted football to grow, and he felt the NFL was dragging its feet with expansion efforts. "I think there was an opportunity, the sport needed to grow" he recalled. "It had gone through a consolidation period and we had seen the great 1958 championship game between the Giants and Colts. There was great national interest in the game and there were a lot of cities frankly that were growing, not all of them had great stadium facilities. But it was beginning to happen. The public was beginning to perceive that this game had national appeal."[5] Bud Adams remembered that at first, the new owners of the AFL were he and his partner, Lamar Hunt. Other owners came on board later. "Well, when we started out, there were two of us. Then we had four more to come in and the last one to come in was Oakland, because Minnesota pulled out, they were in there originally. We even gave them their $25,000 back. We were foolish on that. We thought it was the proper thing to do because they (Minnesota) were going over to the NFL."[6]

One of the new owners who came in was Ralph C. Wilson. Wilson was born in Columbus, Ohio and grew up in Detroit, Michigan. He graduated from the University of Michigan Law School before he enlisted in the Navy during World War II. He served as a minesweep, and received a Commendation Medal. After the war, Wilson went back to being a civilian. He played professional tennis and took over his father's business. Wilson turned the company into Ralph C. Wilson Industries, Inc. and expanded the business into contract-drilling operations, manufacturing, TV and radio stations, construction and insurance.[7] By the late 1950s Ralph Wilson was a wealthy man. One day he read a New York Times article about the new American Football League. Intrigued, Wilson contacted Lamar Hunt. He wanted in. Wilson owned a winter home in Miami, a city the NFL and AFL both considered as a football expansion location. Wilson reached out to the University of Miami and asked them if a new AFL team could play at the university's Orange

Bowl. The school's officials turned him down, because they didn't want any pro-team competing with college football.[8]

Wilson was disappointed by the rebuff. "I was all set to go there, but the University of Miami wouldn't lease the Orange Bowl to me"[9] he told author Scott Pitoniak. "Miami had had bad luck with new football teams. They had a team in the old All-America Conference after World War II. I think it folded around the third quarter of its seventh game. The last thing they wanted was another pro team that might not be able to pay its rent."[10] Wilson was crushed, and he thought his dreams of owning a pro football franchise were over. A few days later, Lamar Hunt called him and told Wilson not to worry about Miami. The new AFL needed an eighth team to balance its schedule, and Hunt gave him a list of possible cities that included St. Louis, Louisville, Cincinnati, Atlanta and Buffalo.[11]

Ralph Wilson asked a sportswriter friend in Detroit to give him some advice. "If you were dumb enough to go into a new football league and you had these five cities to choose from, which one would you pick?"[12] Without missing a beat, the writer told him "Buffalo."[13] Wilson traveled to Buffalo and met with Paul Neville, the managing editor of The Buffalo Evening News. The two men toured the city together, and Neville did his best to persuade the Detroit mogul to choose Buffalo as the place for his new football team. "We had lunch and he said 'Geez, we'd really like to have you put your franchise here,"[14] Wilson remembered. "I said, OK, Paul, here's what I'll do. If your paper will support me for three years, I'll put the franchise here."[15] The two of them shook on it. Wilson was skeptical that the new league would make it, but he was willing to take a risk. "They weren't good odds, but I had always been a risk-taker in business. I really believe in going for it on fourth-and-one," he explained.[16]

Wilson and the other new team owners paid $25,000 each to start a new American Football League franchise. Skeptics nicknamed the new group the "Foolish Club" because who could be foolish enough to think they could compete with the NFL? The new AFL owners were undeterred. They began pioneering innovations that made football more exciting, and they understood how these changes would play on the relatively new medium called television. NFL teams emphasized controlling the ball and relying on the run instead of the pass. AFL quarterbacks threw a lot more passes, and they were willing to risk interceptions to draw viewers in. During the NFL championship game in Dec. 1960 between the Philadelphia Eagles and Green Bay Packers, the two teams passed 55 times for a total of 382 yards. At the AFL championship game on New Year's Day 1961, the Houston Oilers and Los Angeles Chargers passed 73 times for 472 yards. Oilers quarterback Greg Blanda said that "Our goal was to score a lot of points, open up the game and make it more viewable."[17]

Buffalo Bills owner Ralph Wilson (standing 3rd from the left) poses with the other members of the AFL's "Foolish Club" in 1961. Called foolish for taking on the established NFL, the AFL's owners revolutionized the game of football and helped make it the most popular sport in the United States. *Photo courtesy of the American Football Hall of Fame. http://www.remembertheafl.com*

AFL teams used the pass to set up the run, put names on the back of player's jerseys, made the scoreboard clock official (previously, referees had kept time on the field), introduced the two-point conversion and welcomed African-American players to the game. They also began playing games on Thanksgiving Day.[18] The NFL had underestimated the "Foolish Club" and they confirmed this shortsightedness in 1965, when NBC signed a five-year $36 million television deal with the AFL, way more than CBS was paying for NFL games. Ralph Wilson believed the TV contract was a major NFL oversight. "The thing that had made us players was the network television contract we had landed. I think that gave us legitimacy, and I think the NFL had made the cardinal business mistake by underestimating the competition. They became complacent."[19] The NFL owners were quick to retaliate. They told CBS not to give AFL scores during broadcasts. The two leagues also got into a bidding war, trying to lure players from each other's teams. Finally, in the summer of 1966, the two leagues agreed to merge.[20] The "Foolish Club" had the last laugh.

Ralph Wilson kept the Bills in Buffalo from October 1959, when he paid a $25,000 franchise fee to the AFL, until March 25, 2014, when he passed away at the age of 95. Wilson's heirs eventually sold the Bills to Buffalo Sabres owners Terry and Kim Pegula on Sept. 9, 2014 for $1.4 billion, not a bad long-term investment. The Pegulas, like Wilson, plan to keep the Bills in Buffalo for as long as they're around. If Ralph Wilson had been able to set up an AFL franchise in Miami, his first choice, and the University of Miami and the area's politicians had been able to make a deal, his sportswriter friend in Detroit had suggested a different location, or Buffalo News editor Paul Neville hadn't persuaded him, would Buffalo have a pro football team today?

Jeff Miller, author and Bills historian, believes that if Ralph Wilson went to Miami, Buffalo would still get a football team in the AFL or NFL, either in 1960 or as an expansion team in 1966. After that time, Buffalo's window of opportunity closes, because the city was not growing past that point. "Let's go back in history a little bit. Buffalo had a team in the NFL in the 1920s. And in the '30s and '40s there was talk from Bert Bell and George Halas that Buffalo would get a franchise whenever the NFL was going to expand. Buffalo was always considered and at one point there were newspaper articles where Bert Bell, the commissioner of the NFL actually said, we are looking at Buffalo coming into the league. This was in the '40s before the All-American Conference came along and then the All-America Conference comes along and Buffalo's in that so of course, they're not going to be in the NFL but Buffalo was the second highest attended team in the league, but they still weren't accepted into the NFL because…there were a lot of politics going on."

"But I think when you get to the point where it's 1960, Buffalo's a proven football city. If Miami gets the franchise because Ralph Wilson chooses to go there, I think Buffalo gets an expansion team probably in '66. They started in Miami, but… Buffalo definitely becomes an expansion team in '66. And if not, I don't know if they ever would have made into the NFL after that because the NFL was looking for cities that were growing. Buffalo certainly wasn't growing after 1960. So, if they hadn't gotten into the AFL, they probably never would have gotten into the NFL."[21]

Tim Graham, former Buffalo News sports reporter and senior writer at The Athletic, feels that Buffalo had a short window of opportunity in the 1960s to land a football franchise, because once the 1970s came and the region's economy started to really suffer with the loss of heavy industry, the city was not a viable location for an expansion team. It was also too close to other major population centers to make economic sense. "If Ralph doesn't pick Buffalo, as Buffalo continued to shrink as Bethlehem Steel closed, I don't think that Buffalo becomes an attractive expansion market. You think of all the places where the NFL expanded after it merged with the AFL and they were coastal locations: Tampa Bay, Seattle and then getting into that next round of Jacksonville, Carolina. They're going south, they're expanding. True expansion. Not a town that is four hours from Pittsburgh, three hours from Cleveland, four hours from Detroit."[22]

Graham also believes that if Ralph Wilson had been able to get an AFL franchise in Miami, his first choice, the chances of another wealthy business owner choosing Buffalo as a new team's location are slim to none. Wilson lived in Detroit, a near enough Great Lakes city that he could easily commute from. In addition, he picked the city by chance, only because a friend suggested it. Wilson could easily have chosen one of the other cities that Lamar Hunt gave him, St. Louis, Louisville,

Cincinnati or Atlanta, if anyone had made a strong case for them. "Buffalo just does not seem like an attractive market. …If you're the AFL overlords and you're plotting how to start off the AFL, Miami seems like an obvious market. But Buffalo was not. A business associate urged Ralph to try Buffalo. It wasn't the AFL thinking this is in our master plan. It was, OK, Ralph says this is close enough to home, I could come to the games. So, let's say that Ralph gets Miami and they're still looking for the next investor. But he's from Albuquerque or he's from…Birmingham and he's got his money. He's not going to put it in Buffalo. So, you needed to find a guy with the willingness to put it in Buffalo but also close enough to Buffalo… Let's say you did get a guy from Cleveland who has the money…That doesn't mean he's going to put in Buffalo, he might put it in Des Moines…give Chicago another team, put an AFL team in Chicago. It just seems like there are…so many variables there and it just happened to fall right for Buffalo."[23]

The Miami Orange Bowl in 2007. In 1959, new AFL franchise owner Ralph Wilson approached the University of Miami and tried to lease the Orange Bowl for pro football games. Miami was Wilson's first choice, but when university leaders refused, he decided to locate his team in Buffalo. *Photo by Totenkopf. Licensed under the Creative Commons, https://en.wikipedia.org/wiki/Miami_Orange_Bowl#/media/File:Orange_Bowl.jpg*

Sal Maiorana, author and Rochester Democrat and Chronicle sports reporter, agrees with Miller that if Ralph Wilson had bought an AFL franchise in Miami, Buffalo would still have had a chance to get an AFL or NFL franchise later in the 1960s. Buffalo had begun to decline economically during that decade, but the city was still a viable location for a pro football team. "Over the course of the '40s and '50s (the NFL) had kind of bypassed Buffalo. It was already a town that was stuck, it was in decline…the industry was starting to suffer. But I do think that there was enough opportunity in professional football with the NFL expanding at the time in the 1960s. The AFL expanded later in that decade to Cincinnati. So, I think somewhere in the 1960s if it hadn't happened with the original AFL team, I think Buffalo would have gotten a football franchise at some point in the '60s."

"There's no question Buffalo could have had a football franchise in the AFL or the NFL. The NFL, they had a franchise in Minnesota and Dallas both in 1960, and later Atlanta, and New Orleans (as expansion teams in the 1960s). That's four right there. The AFL had Buffalo and Cincinnati. Buffalo or Cincinnati, you could maybe toss a coin for them. Maybe it wouldn't have happened. But I certainly think Buffalo would have had a chance for an AFL or NFL team."[24]

Milt Northrop, Buffalo News sports reporter, points out that there was a strong movement led by local business and political leaders who were trying to bring pro football to Buffalo throughout the 1950s, and they would have continued their efforts even if Ralph Wilson had gone somewhere else. "There were people that were…partly responsible for Ralph coming here in the first place, one being Pat McGroder who later became the vice president of the Bills, he actually was general manager briefly for a while. He was a police commissioner, he was politically connected by a local businessman. Another person was a guy named Paul Neville who was the editor of The Buffalo News. Paul was a big football guy, he was a Notre Dame graduate… I think people like that would have jumped in…Wilson already had the franchise, he put up $25,000. He had some ties in Miami because of the horse racing and vacationed there. But I think somebody would have tried to bring a team here (if Wilson didn't). Now McGroder and other people…were instrumental in the '50s in bringing exhibition games here. Not only exhibition games, actually there were some regular season games played here."[25]

Northrop describes how, during that era, baseball was the dominant sport in the United States and football a distant second. As a result, teams such as the New York Giants of the NFL, who shared space at Yankee Stadium, were often forced to start their season on the road and ended playing in cities like Buffalo. This laid the groundwork for local fans to become interested in the game. "The Giants used to always have a problem in September opening their season…because the Yankees in the '50s were always in the World Series and they (the Giants) played in Yankee Stadium. So, a couple times they got booted out of Yankee Stadium…They used to have to open the season on the road, then one year they…played the Chicago Cardinals. They actually opened the regular season in Buffalo…That happened more than once."[26]

As a result, he believes that local leaders such as McGroder and Neville might have found a different owner and ownership group to bring professional football to Buffalo, if Ralph Wilson had found success in Miami. "I think somebody would have stepped forward, now who would have I have no idea…Perhaps people like the Riches or perhaps the Jacobs or the Knoxes. The people of that era or even the Pastors who had Pepsi and the Bisons… might have stepped forward or put together a group to. It was no sure thing, but there were people here who were trying, who worked to get pro football or some version into Buffalo during the '50s and they probably would have. They helped Ralph(Wilson), they greased the skids here getting a lease on the Rock Pile, getting improvements, expanding capacity there. So, there were some people who were working for pro football in Buffalo."[27]

Matt Sabuda, WBFO sports commentator, feels that Buffalo would have landed a pro football team regardless of whether it was Ralph Wilson or someone else. "I don't know who has a team in Buffalo, but at that time I think it was a foregone conclusion. Even though Wilson wanted the Miami franchise at first…There would have been an NFL team in Buffalo, well I should say an AFL team in Buffalo but who the owner is, that would be the big question mark, that I couldn't tell you. But they were committed to wanting a team in Buffalo in that time frame."[28]

Chris Ostrander, sportswriter for Two in the Box.com, disagrees with other sports pundits who think that if Ralph Wilson didn't come to Buffalo, some other football owner would have. Buffalo hadn't had much luck with pro sports teams in the past, and the city was fortunate that the Bills had an owner who stayed in town through the lean times. Wilson was also blessed with a long life, and he resisted pressure to sell or move the team. Without Wilson, there would be no Buffalo Bills franchise. "At that point (1960) the AHL Bisons weren't around for another five years…There were financial failures that were many. The few pro teams in various sports that were in Buffalo, prior to the '60s, very few of them enjoyed much success. So, I don't think that there would have been a local ownership group…that would have brought the Bills along then nor do I think that you would have caught the lighting a bottle…that you had with Ralph Wilson because of his longevity. And I would even say his stubbornness in terms of really operating the team in a very narrow focus…in terms of the way he operated not only the team but so often voting against things like expansion and relocation. I think he was a good fit for Buffalo as it turns out. I don't think his legacy would have been much different had he gone to Miami instead."

"I think you probably would have seen him run his team pretty similarly to the way he ran the Bills but I can't speak to whether the AFL would have had the same success or not. But I don't know if we'd be talking about having a professional football team at this point had he gone elsewhere."[29]

So, no Ralph Wilson in Buffalo, possibly a different owner or ownership group with an expansion AFL or NFL franchise in Buffalo in the early or mid 1960s. A different owner could have moved the team when Buffalo's economy declined in the later 1960s and '70s, or maybe with Ralph Wilson running an AFL team in Miami, nobody else would have stepped in to start a Buffalo team in the first place. Bills fans can be grateful that Wilson did chose Buffalo after all, even though at times his relationship with many fans was strained. He did threaten to move the team several times during his tenure, but he never followed through with it. Toward the end of his life, Wilson acknowledged that the fans had stuck with the Bills through feast and famine, and he appreciated them for it. "The people here have endured some tough economic times, but they've done a great job supporting the Bills, under the circumstances,"[30] he told author Scott Pitoniak. "The team has given them and me a lot to cheer about through the years."[31] Wilson quipped that "People used to throw their programs at me. Now they're asking me to sign them."[32]

Ralph Wilson stuck it out in Buffalo, when a different owner might have bolted for greener pastures. He pushed for a revenue-sharing system to ensure that the NFL isn't completely dominated by a few big city, corporate rich teams, The smaller markets needed an equal playing field to keep the league viable, he felt. "I think people like the fact that we've had competitive balance through the years. People like to know that an underdog market like a Green Bay or a Buffalo or a Cleveland can compete with the Washington Redskins and New York Giants and Chicago Bears. I'd hate to see the day come when that's not the case."[33]

Wilson hoped his legacy would be that he made life a little brighter, more exciting and interesting for hard-working Western New Yorkers. "There are a lot of people who go through life who don't do anything for anybody. They're born. They live. They're gone. I believe people should make some sort of contribution to make the world better. It doesn't have to be major. It can be minor. I would like to think that by bringing the Bills to Western New York, I've made a contribution to improving the quality of life here. That's how I would like to be remembered."[34]

CHAPTER 5
What if Terry and Kim Pegula Didn't Buy the Buffalo Sabres?

IN THE MID-1960S BUFFALO had a five-year-old American Football League team called the Buffalo Bills. The city had no major league baseball franchises, even though baseball backers made several short-lived attempts to establish a permanent team in the late 1800s and early 1900s.[1] College basketball was also a popular sport, with the "Little Three" Canisius College, Niagara University and St. Bonaventure University competing with each other and entertaining crowds of fans at Memorial Auditorium during Saturday night games.[2]

At the same time, there was a fourth sport that competed for Buffalo sports fans' attention: ice hockey. Western New Yorkers had been captivated by hockey's fast-paced action since the late 1920s, when the Buffalo Bisons (not to be confused with football and baseball teams with the same names) began playing at Fort Erie's Peace Bridge arena.[3] In the 1930s another hockey franchise called the Buffalo Majors played for several seasons at the Broadway Auditorium on the city's East Side.[4] Both the Majors and the Bisons soon went under, victims of the Great Depression. However, they laid the groundwork for Buffalo to land another hockey team that would play when Memorial Auditorium opened on October 14, 1940, a new franchise called the Buffalo Bisons. Unlike the original Bisons, this new minor league team would enjoy long-term success in the International Hockey League, and win the Calder Cup championship five times.[5]

By 1965, Seymour and Northrup Knox, two wealthy and well-connected old money local power brokers, decided it was time for Buffalo to have a big-league hockey team in the National Hockey League. After all, they reasoned, Buffalo had a long hockey history, a large interested fan base, a strong TV market and community leaders who would support a new team.[6] They made a formal application to the National Hockey League for an expansion team, but the NHL rejected their bid. When the Knoxes met with Jim Norris, chairman of the NHL Board of Governors, he told them Buffalo was a bush town and he vowed to never let Buffalo into the league as long as he was involved. Norris had lost money on a grain milling operation he invested in the city, and he let his personal business influence his decision to block the Knoxes' bid.[7]

The Knox brothers brushed off Jim Norris' personal pettiness, and they decided to bide their time and try again. They bought and ran the Buffalo Bisons, the city's minor league hockey team, and waited for a chance to reapply to the NHL in the future. Their opportunity came a few years later, when New York Rangers owner Bill Jennings called Seymour Knox and told him one of the NHL's new expansion teams was a losing franchise, the Oakland Seals. If the Knoxes could turn the Seals around it would prove to the league that they could be successful owners, and make it easier for them to land a new team in Buffalo during the next round of NHL expansions.[8] The Bison's owners jumped at the chance. They agreed to own and operate the Seals in exchange for a new NHL franchise in Buffalo during the next expansion period. The league wouldn't guarantee this but the NHL did name Seymour Knox an alternate governor with veto power over league issues.[9]

Under their new ownership, the Seals had a winning record during the 1968-69 season and clinched the final playoff spot. That sealed the deal with the NHL. After months of negotiations with Seymour and Northrup Knox, on Dec. 1, 1969, the league announced that Buffalo, along with Vancouver, would be awarded a new NHL franchise for the 1970-71 season.[10] The Knoxes had outwitted and outlasted Jim Norris, proven the skeptics wrong and had the last laugh. The Buffalo Sabres were born.

The new owners got the new name through a mail-in contest. The Knoxes asked

Buffalo's hockey fans what they should name the new team, and fans' suggestions were all over the place. Of the 13,000 entries that flooded in, there were some wild and strange choices including the Flying Zeppelins, the Streaks, the Buzzing Bees, the Comets, the Mugwumps and the Herd. In the end, the Knox brothers settled on a name that four people had suggested, the Sabres. Chuck Burr, the team's public relations director, told fans why the owners had picked that title. "A sabre is renowned as a clean, sharp, decisive and penetrating weapon on offense as well as a strong parrying weapon on defense."[11]

Buffalo's Memorial Auditorium during a Sabres home game in 1995. Originally built as a WPA project and opened in 1940, the Aud hosted the minor league hockey Buffalo Bisons from 1940-1970 and the NHL's Buffalo Sabres from 1970-1996. The venue was also the home of the NBA's Buffalo Braves from 1970-1978 and the site for concerts, shows, lacrosse, soccer and college basketball. In 1996 the Sabres moved to Marine Midland Arena, now KeyBank Center. The Aud stood vacant until 2009, when it was demolished. *Photo by Bob Busser.*

Many media experts and pundits, especially in Canada, believed the Sabres would only make it as a team because Buffalo was located on an international border and the franchise would have to be propped up by Canadian fans crossing the Peace Bridge to watch hockey games. Instead, while Canadian attendance was high when the Sabres played opponents like the Leafs and Habs at home, during the first 25 years of the team the Sabres' season ticket base was never more than 13% Canadian.[12] The new franchise's fans had plenty to cheer about in the early years. The Sabres hired the talented, temperamental and colorful former Maple Leafs coach Punch Imlach, who later served as GM. The team won the draft lottery in 1970 and picked the best young junior player in Canada, Gilbert Perreault. Within a few seasons the team's managers acquired fellow French-Canadians Rick Martin and Rene Robert and combined them with Perreault to make the "French Connection" one of the highest scoring offensive lines in Sabres history. New GM Imlach also built up the defense with draft pick Jim Schonfeld and defensive veteran Tim Horton of Tim Horton's fame. By 1975 the Sabres had made it to the Stanley Cup Finals against the Philadelphia Flyers.[13]

1975 would prove to be the high-water mark in Sabres history for a long time. The Sabres lost in the finals to the Philadelphia Flyers, four games to two. They would continue to make the playoffs for the rest of the 1970s, but couldn't reach the finals again. The Blue and Gold remained a winning team and the Sabres were playoff contenders most seasons in the 1980s and '90s. Even so, changes were afoot. Buffalo's Memorial Auditorium had been the home of the minor league Buffalo Bisons from 1940-1970 and served as hockey headquarters for the Sabres since then.[14] However, by the last decade of the 20th century, the nature of pro sports was changing. Team owners wanted lucrative revenue from corporate box seats and suites. The Aud was a beloved icon, but it was built in the New Deal Era for the common people, not the wealthy corporate bigwigs.

As a result, on April 14, 1996, the Buffalo Sabres played their last game at the Aud against the Hartford Whalers. Fittingly, the Sabres won 4-1, and captain Pat LaFontaine shot one last puck in the net before skating off the ice. Team owner Seymour Knox III said after the game that he attempted to be stoic. "I tried my best, but I think probably some (tears) snuck out. It was an emotional evening."[15] It was Knox's last game at the Aud, too because he died of cancer a month later.

The Sabres moved a few blocks downtown to brand new Marine Midland Arena, close to the Inner Harbor and the Buffalo and Erie County Naval Park. The new arena had the spanking new construction looks, open spaces and the required corporate suites and luxury boxes. However, the new facility lacked the character and soul of the Sabres' old digs. During their inaugural season at the Arena, former coach Joe Crozier reminisced about the Sabres' old skating grounds. "The Aud had charisma" he said. "It was a smaller rink and the people were closer to the ice, so you had a lot going for you in that place. There was so much enthusiasm in that building. I remember I'd come in and there would be people lined up in the lobby waiting to buy tickets (including the author's uncle and his friend, who once camped out all night to be the first in line). The fans were great; they really helped us. There was a hell of a difference for us playing at home with those people behind us."[16]

The Sabres' time at the Aud had passed, Seymour Knox had passed, and soon Knox ownership would pass. After the 1997-98 season the Knox heirs sold the Buffalo Sabres to local cable TV businessmen John, Tim, Michael and James Rigas of Adelphia Cable Communications.[17] The Rigas family had built a small regional cable company based in Coudersport, Pennsylvania into the 6th largest cable TV provider in the United States.[18]

At first, the new ownership change didn't affect the team's playoff prospects. In fact, as it turned out the 1998-99 season was the best one the Sabres had since 1975. The team made the Stanley Cup Finals for the first time in 24 years and played the Dallas Stars for the Cup. During the third overtime period of Game 6, Dallas Stars winger Brett Hull put his foot in the Sabres' goal crease and shot the puck in the net.[19] At that time, it was against NHL rules for players to put their foot in the goal crease and shoot the puck.[20] However, league officials and NHL Commissioner Gary Bettman allowed the goal to stand, and awarded Dallas the Stanley Cup.

A few years after this blow, in 2002, Buffalo fans were shocked to learn that

John, Tim, Michael and James Rigas of Adelphia Cable were forced to declare bankruptcy. The Rigases were arrested and charged with corporate fraud and embezzlement. The NHL had to step in and run the team until the league could find a buyer.[21] Sabres fans began to worry about who might buy the franchise, because a new owner might not be as committed to keeping the team in Buffalo as the Knox family and the Rigases had been. With the Sabres' future in Western New York in doubt, game attendance and season ticket sales plummeted. By March of 2003, there were only 5,800 season ticket holders and game day attendance averaged 12,500 for an 18,700-seat arena. The Sabres' TV ratings were a terrible 3.5 percent share.[22]

That same month, a sports savior stepped in to keep the team in Buffalo. Rochester billionaire B. Thomas Golisano, founder and owner of Paychex Inc., agreed to purchase the Sabres franchise from the NHL for $92 million. Golisano recalled later that he was not a hockey fan, and he'd only been to three games in his life. However, he became interested in buying the Sabres in 2002, when he was running for governor of New York State. "I traveled to Buffalo quite a bit" Golisano told Rochester Business Journal writer Thomas Adams, and "I started hearing the story about the Buffalo Sabres, that the community was afraid that the team was going to leave Western New York, that the arena would go dark and the psyche of the community and the economics of the community would all be affected."[23] Golisano went over to look at the new arena, and the media picked up on his interest and began touting him as a potential new owner. The Sabres announced the team's sale to Golisano on March 3, 2003. Golisano held a press conference in downtown Buffalo but refused to invite any politicians to the event because he said they had given him a hard time.[24]

Once he had the reigns, Golisano would leave his mark by running the team as a business. He cut Sabres payroll by a third. Cutting employees wasn't popular, but Golisano did something else that was popular, cutting ticket prices. The Sabres introduced variable ticket pricing, with higher demand games against teams like

Toronto and Montreal being more expensive, but other games against less popular opponents being cheaper. The overall effect lowered average ticket prices, and sold out games became a common event in an arena that had struggled to fill seats just a few years earlier. However, Golisano made a major policy decision that caused talented players to leave Buffalo and sign with teams that paid better salaries. "We can't lose money" he declared. "If the Buffalo Sabres pay to the salary cap, we lose money. We're just under the salary cap, and hopefully we'll break even. If we make the playoffs, maybe we'll be fortunate enough to make a few dollars."[25]

Golisano's insistence that the Sabres couldn't pay to the salary cap had unintended consequences. In 2006 and 2007 the team made it to the Eastern Conference Finals. Led by talented co-captains Danny Briere and Chris Drury, backed by stellar goaltender Ryan Miller and a depth of good offensive and defensive players, the Sabres looked like a team that was arguably as good as the glory days of the French Connection Era. In the second round of the playoffs against the New York Rangers, the series was tied at two games each. In Game 5 in Buffalo, the Rangers broke a scoreless game in the third period and scored a goal with 3:29 left. Just when it looked like New York would take a crucial 3-2 series lead, Chris Drury scored on Henrik Lundqvist with 7.7 seconds left to force an overtime. Maxim Afinogenov then made the game-winning goal thanks to Drury's last minute tie. The Sabres would go on to win the series before losing to the Ottawa Senators in the Conference Finals.[26]

Normally, any hockey team would want to resign players like Drury and Briere, who would become free agents after the 2006-07 season. In fact, Drury was willing to agree to a four-year deal with the Sabres for $21.5 million, but GM Darcy Regier never offered it to him for signing. Chris Drury felt that the Sabres didn't want him to stay, and he shopped around for other offers. The New York Rangers gave him a five-year deal for $35.25 million, and on July 1, 2007, Drury headed to New York City. Co-captain Danny Briere joined the Philadelphia Flyers with an eight-year, $52 million offer, something Regier and managing partner Larry Quinn were unable or unwilling to spend. As author Sal Maiorana put it "Just like that, two players who'd scored a combined 69 goals and 164 points in 2006-2007 were gone: Drury, the heart and soul of the team, and Briere, its' most talented offensive player . Given their skill, their leadership, and their popularity with the fans, it was a dark, dark summer day in Buffalo."[27] Darcy Regier admitted that "We're going to be less competitive without Danny Briere and Chris Drury. But the sky's not falling. This is a good hockey club. We'll be good. We'll figure out a way-somehow, some way-to be better."[28] More than a decade later, the Sabres are still figuring.

Losing Chris Drury and Danny Briere was a major blow for the franchise. The Sabres would miss the playoffs for the next two seasons. In 2009, owner Tom Golisano moved to Florida to escape paying taxes in New York State.[29] As Golisano transitioned his interests and his home outside Western New York, fans began to worry that Golisano wanted to sell the team, just a few short years after he bought it. The Sabres owner denied the rumors, and he reassured fans and the local media in the summer of 2010 that nothing was set in stone, but he would probably still own the Sabres in five or even 10 years.[30] Boston Globe sportswriter Kevin Paul Dupont didn't believe Golisano, and he floated two names as potential new owners. The first was Jim Balsillie, who got rebuffed by the NHL when he tried to buy the Phoenix Coyotes and move them to Toronto's suburbs. The second name was Terry Pegula. Dupont thought that unlike Balsillie, Pegula would be a good potential owner. "He's the guy who forked over the $88 million gift for Penn State to build a rink and fund scholarships for Division 1 hockey. Pegula's wife, Kim, is from suburban Buffalo, a good sign for the locals. No one ever wants to leave the Buff."[31]

Dupont got one detail wrong. Kim Pegula was from suburban Rochester,[32] not Buffalo. But she was a native Western New Yorker, always a good sign for worried Buffalo fans. Her husband, Terry was a Pennsylvania native who graduated from Penn State with a degree in petroleum engineering and worked for Getty Oil before starting his own oil and later natural gas fracking company, East Resources,

Inc. in 1983. Pegula borrowed $7,500 from friends and family to get started.[33] Oil and natural gas exploration brought Terry Pegula to Olean, New York in the rural Southern Tier south of Buffalo. Pegula met his wife Kim at a bar in Olean, where she was applying to become a waitress. Terry offered her a job at his company instead, and their relationship developed from there.[34]

Pegula would not only meet his wife in Olean, but the Pennsylvania native would also become a hockey fan. Pegula liked hockey so much he became the assistant coach of the Olean Arrows Mites, a children's junior hockey team. Pegula's interest in hockey also led him to become a Buffalo Sabres fan. Head coach Ryan Jordan remembered that "Terry already had Sabres season tickets, and I soon got them. We never missed a game and usually rode (to Buffalo) together."[35] Pegula told a business partner a few years earlier that if he ever had more than two nickels to his name, he'd buy the Buffalo Sabres someday.[36] Terry Pegula would manage a small company for many years, that, while it made more than two nickels, didn't make him enough to purchase a hockey franchise. All of that changed in 2010, the same year Tom Golisano denied that he wanted to sell the Sabres. That year, Pegula sold East Resources, with more than 600,000 acres of natural gas rich land, to Royal Dutch Shell for an unbelievable sum of $4.7 billion.[37] Now the Pennsylvania fracking tycoon had more than enough cash to own the Sabres, if a certain Rochester payroll mogul was willing to part with them.

On Feb. 1, 2011, the Sabres stunned everyone by announcing that Tom Golisano had agreed to sell the Buffalo Sabres franchise and related companies to Terry Pegula. The sale was subject to NHL approval, but Pegula impressed the league owners with his passion and commitment.[38] The NHL quickly approved the sale to Pegula for $189 million. Golisano had bought a struggling hockey team for $92 million and cleared a profit of $65 million, because according to Forbes, the Sabres had lost $32 million during Golisano's ownership.[39] Terry Pegula held a press conference in Buffalo on February 22nd, and the new owner was quite a contrast to Tom Golisano, who once said "You would be amazed at the owners of National Hockey League teams, and other sports teams, that don't mind losing money. They're so dedicated to the concept of potentially winning, they're willing to do almost anything relative to that effect."[40]

Golisano could have been talking about Pegula, who told a room full of reporters at his first media event that "If I want to make some money, I'll go drill a gas well. I don't need to make it in the hockey business. Starting today, there will be no financial mandates on the Buffalo Sabres' hockey department."[41] Golisano had made decisions based on how they reflected the bottom line. For Pegula, the Sabres would make decisions "Based on winning the Stanley Cup and what is right for the fan base and the team."[42] For fans who never got over the Sabres letting Chris Drury and Danny Briere go, Pegula told them "Darcy (Regier) will run a hockey department that I have previously said will have no financial mandates. We're cutting the chains off, and he's free to run with whatever he wants to do."[43]

Hockey legend Gilbert Perreault and new Buffalo Sabres owner Terry Pegula hold up a No. 4 Pegula jersey, Feb. 22, 2011. Pegula was the 4th owner in franchise history, and bought the Sabres from Rochester, NY business mogul B. Thomas Golisano. *Photo by AP.*

Terry and his wife Kim have remained team owners in the years since, with mixed results. The Sabres haven't consistently made the playoffs or won a Stanley Cup, which Terry Pegula said was the team's mission starting the day he bought them.[44] The Sabres have gone through several coaches and GMs, with many fans feeling that the Pegulas keep dead wood around longer than they need to. They've spent lavishly on player salaries and downtown Buffalo, building a state-of-the-art HarborCenter with an Academy of Hockey and new Sabres offices across from KeyBank Center. They've put up statues that immortalized the French Connection. They even stepped up and bought the Buffalo Bills, the area's other pro sports team, to prevent the franchise from leaving Western New York. What if they hadn't? What if Terry Pegula never moved to Olean, met his future wife Kim, started a fracking company, sold it for a huge profit and used that money to buy the Buffalo Sabres? How would the team fare today?

Matt Sabuda, WBFO sports commentator, feels that if the Pegulas hadn't bought the franchise, a different local owner would have made a bid. Buffalo is one of the major TV markets for hockey in the United States. Even when the Sabres aren't playing, for example during the Stanley Cup Finals, Buffalo fans follow hockey closely. The NHL would have found a local buyer for the Sabres if Golisano wanted to sell the franchise and Terry Pegula hadn't entered the scene, because of this reason. "I think the Sabres would have been all right. I don't see the Sabres leaving. I think another ownership group would have stepped in. What that would have looked like is anybody's guess but the Sabres represent…one of the cornerstone United States markets for the NHL. If you ever take a look or even do some digging on this part of it from a ratings perspective Buffalo has always had some of the highest ratings for NHL hockey even when the Sabres aren't in it."

"If you even look at Stanley Cup Finals, year in year out there were even games this year that Buffalo was number two ahead of Pittsburgh…in the finals. So not Pittsburgh, Washington when they were in the finals…It's something that they are consistently at the top of the rankings when it comes to TV viewership. So, I think the NHL would have wanted to see a solid ownership group still step in if Terry and Kim Pegula weren't that ownership group."[45]

Tim Graham, former Buffalo News sports reporter and senior writer at The Athletic, is not sure who would have bought the Sabres if the Pegulas hadn't come on the scene, but Tom Golisano was looking to sell, and it's anyone's guess who would have purchased them, if Terry and Kim Pegula didn't suddenly appear when they did. "Golisano viewed it as an investment after the initial lure. He admitted he didn't know anything about hockey. He was from Rochester and didn't know how to say the word Amerks. He always called them the Uh-MERKS. Every time he would talk about the Uh-MERKS. Let's not forget about how good the Uh-MERKS are doing down there. Once the novelty wore off and he stopped coming to the games it was all about an investment...An investment doesn't pay off until you sell it, of course. So, I don't think he would have held on to it...At some point he was going to flip it."[46]

Graham added that Golisano enjoyed being known as the hero who came to rescue when the previous owners, the Rigas family went to jail and the NHL need-ed a buyer. However, when the novelty wore off and Golisano's policy of not ne-gotiating with players in season cost the Sabres talented stars like Danny Briere and Chris Drury, the Rochester accounting mogul starting looking for a way out. "It used to be you couldn't say a bad word about Tom Golisano, but after those back-to-back Conference Finals years and Drury and Briere leave... Brian Camp-bell left...Jay McKee, popular veterans. They had this policy...of not negotiating in season was their big thing. They would wait till the end of the season and then they would lose a really good player for a contract that was astronomically more than they could have gotten them for during the season. Had they negotiated in season they could have gotten a player for four years and 18 million just to stay and then the player hits free agency and signs for five years, twenty-six million. And then the fans say well we couldn't afford that anyway, so it's become sour grapes."

"No, you could have afforded it if you had been more proactive. Instead you end up saying goodbye to Briere, Drury, Brian Campbell, three all-stars right there. You get held hostage by Vanek. So, the PR had really turned on Tom Golisano. He wasn't the exalted owner of the Sabres anymore like he was. So, I think he was starting to lose his attraction to being a pro sports owner."[47]

Sal Maiorana, author and Rochester Democrat and Chronicle sports reporter, believes that if Terry and Kim Pegula hadn't bought the Sabres, there's a good chance the team might not be in Buffalo today. The Pegulas were instrumental in ensuring that both Buffalo pro sports teams stayed in Buffalo, even though fans haven't always been pleased with the Sabres and Bills' winning records. "Just from my perception...in the industry that I have covered for the Sabres in the past, I think that if the Pegulas hadn't bought the team it could have gone out of town. Again, it totally depends on who else is in the market to buy the franchise. Hockey was certainly Terry Pegula's passion. He bought the Bills to keep them in town, but he really had a passion for hockey. He was a season ticket holder. He told the story. He wanted to come in and save the team, and he did. I think everyone in Buffalo is thankful. I think everyone's frustrated... They haven't done very well. It hasn't been much of a team to watch for seven years. People have had plenty of things to say about the Pegulas. But they've done great things for the city of Buffalo and Western New York. And we have a lot to be thankful for, because...both teams could have, could have been gone from Buffalo if not for their arrival."[48]

Chris Ostrander, sportswriter for Two in the Box.com, feels that if the Pegulas didn't buy the Sabres, Tom Golisano would still be running the team like a business, with no lavish spending on players, HarborCenter or One Buffalo. "We're probably pretty much the same place that we were in all of those seasons, kind of the post Drury-Briere seasons...where the Sabres...occupied that same status as the drought Bills did, being OK but not great. Just not happy with being mediocre but at the very least maybe accepting that fate because Golisano was never going to spend to the cap. I don't even think he was the type of owner that we see in the NHL where there typically are teams that budget, that operate an internal budget rather than the cap but maybe make exceptions when they want to keep their stars. I don't think they would have been one of those teams that we saw where they kept Vanek because they had to but they were very, very quick to deal old guys like Brian Campbell away. A great example."

"We would have seen plenty of favorite players move out before they'd recommit to their time as they did in Buffalo. So, I still think he'd (Golisano) be their owner. I don't think he would have explored the sale of the team but I also don't think the Sabres would be players for big talent. I also don't think that we would have Jack Eichel, Rasmus Dahlin, etc. because short of a really miraculous lottery win the Sabres would have occupied the 7th to 15th place in the draft…We would be looking at a very vanilla, average hockey team that maybe catches lightning in a bottle and has a good playoff run but ultimately just kind of exists, as I feel like they did in terms of talent under Golisano's ownership."[49]

Paul Wieland, author and former Sabres public relations director, thinks that if Tom Golisano still owned the team, the Sabres would have been better off. Anything Golisano has been involved in has been a success. The Pegulas, in his opinion, have produced a losing product and are in over their heads. Wieland is not impressed with the Pegula's leadership, to say the least. "Oh, I think they'd (the Sabres) be a lot better. I think the Pegulas couldn't run a one car funeral. They're terrible owners, they have no idea what they're doing, they had Patty LaFontaine in there. And then they hired a couple of their buddies and gave them vice president titles and told LaFontaine he should report to these guys. That's why he's gone…But they don't know what they're doing. And then they let the team tank for two years. What an embarrassment, tank for two straight years! And yet they raised the prices for the tickets each year. They didn't give any money back for American League teams. I think you could have hired Tweedle Dee and Tweedle Dum to own the Sabres they would be better than they are under the Pegulas that's for sure."

"The guy was an engineer out of Penn State who discovered a way to make money fracking. They might be great community citizens. They gave a lot of money to Penn State, wonderful. But he's running a hockey franchise and he's selling entertainment and he's asking people to pay major league prices. He's supposed to put out a major league product and he took two years to drive it into the ground. He knows as much about running a professional sports team as I know about running New York City ballet."

"Golisano bought it (the Sabres) for peanuts. He picked it up for 40 million plus I'm assuming about 60 million in outstanding obligations. And then he sold it for $180 million. Three or four years later made $80 million on it to the Pegulas. Yeah, not too bad. Tom Golisano is a sharp operator. I think they'd be better (if Golisano still owned the team) because anything he stays into he makes big time. Whatever business he's gotten into they work. When he bought it I'm sure he knew he could turn some bucks on it. But if he stays with it, a couple of companies that he has are extremely successful. The reason is that he's pretty dynamic, he's a pretty good corporate leader. I think they'd be better."[50]

John Krieger, sportswriter for Hockey Central.com, believes Buffalo is lucky the Pegulas came on the scene and kept both major sports franchises from leaving Western New York. They've done a lot to rebuild and refurbish downtown Buffalo, and even if their sports efforts haven't had immediate results in the win column, they'll eventually get there. "They kind of just take Buffalo up from not a bad situation but not a bright future. They ...revitalized it and it's taken some time and we've seen that it wasn't great right away. But even what they're doing within the whole city it's been unreal. They've pretty much got every professional sports team under their name which is awesome. I'm loving the whole One Buffalo thing that they've got going on bringing people together, getting all the other sports and recognition...They've really shown that they do care about the city and the fans and how passionate we are. I think they really just want to give Buffalo fans what they deserve. And I do believe we're on the right track with that."

"If the Pegulas didn't buy the team when they did we might not even have an

NHL team right now. And honestly, we might not have an NFL team either. That was kind of a bit of a worry. I know they were thinking about moving to Toronto which everybody (there) would have liked to see, losing our football team and our NHL team. We might have been the Vegas Knights, you never know. But I'm definitely glad that the Pegulas purchased both teams when they did."[51]

Tim Graham agrees with Maiorana and Krieger that Terry and Kim Pegula buying both major sports franchises in Buffalo was a huge unexpected gift for the region. The Pegulas came out of nowhere to keep both teams in Buffalo within a few short years. It's fortunate that Terry Pegula was waiting in the wings when Tom Golisano wanted to sell. "Nobody even knew who Pegula was, right? Maybe you get (Jim) Balsillie. He steps in and they let Balsillie buy the team, but then Balsillie wanted to have a team in Hamilton. I don't know if the NHL would have allowed that to happen but…there are always some guys out there who want a sports team. But it's weird with hockey, these guys come out of nowhere it seems like…and… thankfully for Western New York, Terry Pegula emerged out of nowhere because you're talking about the next owner of the Buffalo Bills. Two days before Terry Pegula buys the Sabres nobody knew who Terry Pegula was. You could have asked a hundred people in Buffalo who Terry Pegula was, not one of them could have answered the question. As soon as he buys the Sabres, wait a minute. We've got a guy with all this money with ties to us and he's right here in our own backyard. And then all of a sudden, when Ralph dies, where'd this guy come from? Thankfully he emerged or else who knows what would have happened with either team."[52]

With no Terry Pegula selling East Resources Inc. to Royal Dutch Shell for $4.7 billion in 2010 and using it to buy the Sabres, possibly the team would still be a lackluster franchise under Tom Golisano's continued ownership. Or possibly Golisano would have sold the Sabres to an out-of-town owner who moved the team to a location like Winnipeg, which received the old Atlanta Thrashers team, or Las Vegas, with its new Golden Knights. Golisano might have learned from his mistake letting Briere and Drury leave, and realized that he had to spend money to make money in the NHL. Maybe another local owner would have stepped up, or a Western New York native who did well elsewhere and wanted to come back and own a hockey team.

Owning the Sabres is a fantasy that many local fans contemplate, especially when they see the Sabres leadership make decisions that in hindsight are short-sighted, that they wouldn't make if they were in charge. However, most fans live paycheck to paycheck, and don't have $189 million sitting around to buy a hockey franchise. They only hope that someday they can sing, as author Sal Maiorana put it in his dedication page in 100 Things Sabres Fans Should Know & Do Before They Die, "You know we're gonna win that Cup; you know we're gonna win that Stanley Cup; me and the Buffalo Sabres, yeah, yeah, yeah, and have it actually happen."[53]

CHAPTER 6
What if the Buffalo Sabres Didn't Tank to Draft Jack Eichel During the 2014-15 Season?

DURING THE 2014-15 SEASON, some sports pundits criticized the Buffalo Sabres' managers for allegedly losing intentionally to win one of two eligible NHL draft picks, Connor McDavid and Jack Eichel. Thirty years earlier, the Pittsburgh Penguins faced the same media criticism. In the early 1980s, the Penguins were in trouble. The team had the NHL's worst record in both the 1982-83 and 1983-84 seasons. Combined with Pittsburgh's weakening steel industry that was closing mills and shedding jobs, fans weren't coming to the games and the franchise faced financial difficulties. It looked to many Penguins observers that the team might fold.[1]

In January 1984, the Penguins took a road trip to Montreal. While in Montreal, Penguins coach Louis Angotti, GM Edward Johnston and broadcaster Mike Lange decided to go to a junior hockey game. The three men were captivated by a young player named Mario Lemieux. "Everybody was trying to stop him, and I think he had five breakaways"[2] Angotti remembered.

A few days later, Johnston told Angotti the two of them needed to find a way to draft Lemieux, the No. 1 pick that year, by any means necessary. "When we sat down to see what we had to do to get the first draft choice, E.J. (Eddie Johnston) said it would cost us both our jobs"[3] the coach remembered. Angotti agreed with his boss that it was the right move for the struggling franchise. At that time, there was no draft lottery, so whichever team finished last in the standings got to choose the No. 1 draft choice. The coach set to work to tank during the rest of the 1983-84 season to ensure the Penguins would get Lemieux. Angotti recalled that he would put the wrong players on the ice during special teams situations or play his 4th line against opposing teams' stars. One time he pulled starting goaltender Roberto Romano in a game where the Pens were leading and Pittsburgh ended up losing.[5]

When the Penguins were doing well in a game, it was harder to try to lose than win. Johnston wanted Angotti to sabotage any efforts to pick up points in the standings, and his coach often found it difficult. "If the game started off badly, there wasn't much for me to do. It was the games where we were competitive and looked like we were going to win where I was in position to put us in position to lose. The only thing you could do is manipulate your bench, use whatever you had on your bench to put yourself in a position to lose." Lou Angotti knew he was tanking to get a star player, but it went against all his instincts as a coach. He felt that he was working against his own players, who didn't want to lose any games. "I can honestly say the players who came in to work every day gave all they had. That was the tough part. I was playing against them. It was me against them, them against me. They were trying to go out and win, and I was using them to lose."[6]

During the end of the 1983-84 season, the Penguins were competing with the New Jersey Devils for last place in the standings. The only difference was, unlike Penguins GM Eddie Johnston, Devils GM Max McNab refused to tank, even if Mario Lemieux was at stake. "There was a principle involved" he recalled. "It would have made me sick to my stomach to do something to lose games. It wasn't even a possibility (of getting Lemieux) if it took losing hockey games or bringing up a minor league goalie."[7] Johnston couldn't disagree more. During one game where the Pens were up 3-1 he burst into Angotti's office to demand what he was doing. Pittsburgh would lose the game 6-3. The Penguins lost 18 of the last 21 games of the season, and finished last in the standings to draft Lemieux.[8] The Devils would draft Kirk Muller at No. 2.[9] For Johnston, it was worth the sacrifice to get the No. 1 pick. Many years later, the former GM asked writer Joe Starkey rhetorically if it was right to win an extra game or two at the end of the season and lose Mario Lemieux.[10]

Eddie Johnston had predicted that he and coach Lou Angotti could lose their jobs over tanking. He was right about Angotti, who wouldn't return the next season and never coached in the NHL again.[11] Johnston, the mastermind behind the Lemieux tank, didn't get a pink slip from the Pens. He stayed as Penguins GM until 1988, when he left Pittsburgh to become the Hartford Whalers general manager from 1989 to 1992. Even while he was in Hartford, Johnston was accused of helping the Pens. He traded Whalers captain Ron Francis and defenseman Ulf Samuelsson to the Penguins in 1991 as part of a six-player deal. These players, along with Mario Lemieux, were instrumental in helping the Penguins win two back-to-back Stanley Cup championships in 1991 and 1992. The Penguins' owner forgave Johnston for the tank and hired him as head coach from 1993-1997, when he moved to the assistant GM position. He stayed there until 2006, when he became president of hockey operations, and finally retired in 2009.[12] Tanking for Lemieux may have ended Lou Angotti's hockey career, but it made Johnston's, and it helped turn the Pittsburgh Penguins into an NHL dynasty.

Thirty years after Eddie Johnston hatched a plan to tank to draft Mario Lemieux, another struggling team in another northern city was facing a similar situation. The Buffalo Sabres had never recovered from losing Daniel Briere and Chris Drury in 2007, and the team had made the playoffs only once since then, in 2011. By the beginning of the 2013-14 season the Sabres were in terrible shape. After missing the playoffs for two straight years and finishing the previous season with the NHL's worst record of 21-21-6, in the fall of 2013 Buffalo would win only four of the team's first twenty games. The Sabres had fired coach Lindy Ruff on February 20, 2013,[13] and as it became clear that the something else had to change, owner Terry Pegula sacked both interim coach Ron Rolston and longtime GM Darcy Regier on November 13th.[14] Pegula hired former Sabres player Pat LaFontaine to be the president of hockey operations and brought back former coach Ted Nolan to coach the Sabres again. Both of these hires were popular moves. La-La-La-LaFontaine was the Sabres' high-scoring former captain and Ted Nolan was a beloved figure in Sabreland.

On January 9, 2014, Pegula found a new general manager in Tim Murray, the Ottawa Senators' former assistant GM. Murray had a reputation for being decisive, something that many fans and sportswriters accused Darcy Regier of not being. "I would consider myself somewhat aggressive. I don't think it takes you two days to make a decision or two weeks to make a decision,"[15] Murray told the local media at his first press conference. That aggressiveness might have been a little too much for Pat LaFontaine, because he suddenly quit on March 1st, soon after Murray traded captain Steve Ott and goalie Ryan Miller to the St. Louis Blues.[16] Coach Ted Nolan became visibly upset and sounded like he would quit, too. "Right now is not about my contract. It's about the situation that just happened. It's about what transpired in this organization, what happened to a very dear friend and I will leave it at that."[17] Murray was willing to let Nolan decide. "If he wants to be here, I want him to be our coach."[18] Pat LaFontaine had joined the New York Islanders in an advisory role eight years before and quit just as suddenly. Nolan didn't quit, and when the Blues were eliminated in the playoffs, trading Ott and Miller looked like the right decision.[19]

In spite of Murray's moves, the Sabres kept losing. They finished the 2013-14 season 21-51-10, the second worst record in franchise history.[20] The Sabres couldn't get any worse, however, unlike the situation in Pittsburgh in 1984, where GM Eddie Johnston and coach Lou Angotti quietly conspired to tank to draft Mario Lemieux, this time many Sabres fans wanted to lose for another season. If the team finished dead last in the standings one more time, Buffalo was guaranteed a first-round pick, or if the Sabres lost the first round, a guaranteed second-round pick. The top two picks available in the 2015 NHL Draft were generational talents, Connor McDavid and Jack Eichel.[21] However, in contrast to Lou Angotti, Ted Nolan didn't want to tank. The coach told ESPN writer Pierre LeBrun that the idea of tanking was insulting. It was hard enough to win normally. Planning to lose, in Nolan's view, made no sense.[22]

Nolan was against tanking, and Tim Murray also publicly denied that the Sabres were tanking. However, his actions spoke louder than words. After the 2013-14 season, the NHL changed the draft rules to give every team in the league a chance to draft the No. 1 pick. Sabres GM Tim Murray opposed any draft lottery change, and he shared his opposition with other GMs during a meeting in June 2014.[23] The other GMs ignored his protests and modified the draft rules anyway. When the Sabres had a fourteen-game losing streak in December and January, the normally aggressive and decisive GM sat back and did nothing.[24] In February, Murray recalled defenseman Mark Pysyk from the Rochester Amerks, the Sabres' farm team. Pysyk played three games, the Sabres went 2-0-1, and the new defenseman scored a goal. Back to Rochester he went.[25] After Nolan said that Tyler Myers was "one of those guys you build your team around"[26] Murray traded him.

As the season went on, a growing divide opened up between the majority of the fans, who supported the tank, and a minority of anti-tankers, among them Buffalo News sportswriters Mike Harrington and Bucky Gleason. Harrington had attacked the tank so often in his columns that he gave up editorializing about it. "The Sabres have tanked spectacularly and my feelings have been made crystal clear on these pages, so there's no need to belabor them anymore,"[27] he wrote on February 1st. The tanking and anti-tanking split entered a new and intense phase on March 26, 2015, when the Sabres hosted the Arizona Coyotes. The two teams were racing to the bottom to finish last. If the Coyotes won, Buffalo was one game closer to drafting McDavid or Eichel. Hearing Sabres fans cheer for Arizona was too much for Buffalo News sportswriter Bucky Gleason. "Every team in every league in every game should be doing whatever it can to win every day,"[28] he declared after Arizona beat Buffalo in overtime, 4-3.

The tank was hard for Sabres players to take, too. Defensemen Mike Weber said after the loss to Arizona that "They cheer when they score to win the game. I don't know. I don't even know what to say. This is extremely frustrating for us."[29] The Sabres may have been frustrated, and writers like Gleason and Harrington openly opposed the tank. However, the majority of Sabres fans didn't see things that way.

On the same day the Coyotes played the Sabres in a rematch in Arizona on March 30th, local news station WIVB.com conducted an online poll that asked "Do you still want the Buffalo Sabres to tank?" 87% of respondents said yes, 10% said no and 3% were undecided.[30] One fan, Frank Taberski of Williamsville, expressed many fans' feelings when he explained "I love the Sabres, but how are you going to pass up on a generational player?"[31] Eddie Johnston would have agreed.

The Sabres won the rematch, 4-1, which gave Buffalo 50 points with six games remaining while Arizona had 54 points with five games left. On April 1st, the Sabres hosted the Toronto Maple Leafs. Normally Sabres and Leafs fans would be openly hostile toward each other, but that night it seemed like a Toronto home game. In spite of their lack of fan support, the Sabres beat the Leafs to bring them within two points of Arizona. After playing terribly all season, the Sabres suddenly started to come alive, almost as if the players wanted to sabotage the tank. On April 3rd, the Chicago Blackhawks came to town. The Hawks had recently won two Stanley Cups, and they were tough to beat. A lot of people were there to support South Buffalo's Patrick Kane, and with the tank going on, it was like home ice advantage for the visitors. It should have been an easy Chicago win, but the Sabres refused to buckle.

The game started off with two unanswered Blackhawks goals in the 1st period. Buffalo came back in the second period and halved the Hawks' lead to make it 2-1. Early in the 3rd period Johan Larsson tied the score with a Sabres power play. Then with seven minutes left, Marcus Foligno scored to give the Sabres a 3-2 lead. The tank looked like it was doomed. Buffalo would tie with Arizona, and the chances of Buffalo drafting a generational talent like Connor McDavid or Jack Eichel were slipping away. But the game wasn't over yet. The Chicago Blackhawks would show why they were Stanley Cup champions. Blackhawks captain Jonathan Toews scored a goal with 1:43 remaining to tie the game. Then, incredibly with 56 seconds to go, Toews skated down on a two- on-one and snapped the puck past Sabres goaltender Anders Lindback to make it 4-3 Blackhawks.[32] Toews had scored two goals within 47 seconds to keep the Sabres from derailing the tank.

Even after the Blackhawks win, the tank would go down to a nail-biting, stomach churning finish. The New York Islanders beat Buffalo 3-0 that Saturday on Long Island. Two hours later the Coyotes won their game against San Jose 5-3. Arizona widened its lead over the Sabres with four extra points in the standings. Since there were only three games left, one more Sabres loss or Coyotes win would cement the Sabres in 30th place. On Monday night, the Sabres hosted the Carolina Hurricanes, and won 4-3 to give them two points, and one more Buffalo win would tie them with Arizona. The Sabres had to lose their last game in Columbus against the Blue Jackets, or else the tank would be history. Sabres players gave every indication that they were playing to win in their season closer. Columbus scored first, to make it 1-0, but the Sabres quickly answered back to tie the game 2:25 into the 1st period. Matt Calvert got a goal for Columbus at the 9:35 mark of the 1st to take the lead. The Blue Jackets would keep that lead throughout the 2nd period, but Sabres captain Brian Gionta scored on a power play goal to tie the game 2-2 with 58.4 seconds left in the second. The third period dragged on with a tied game until with 9:25 remaining, Cam Atkinson scored a goal to take a 3-2 Columbus lead. Tankers could not finally relax, until, with 9.7 seconds to go, Boone Jenner shot the puck into the Sabres' empty net to clinch a 4-3 Blue Jackets victory.[33]

The tank was over. Sabres fans could finally take it easy knowing that their team was guaranteed either Connor McDavid or Jack Eichel. On April 18th, the NHL held their draft lottery at Sportsnet Studios in Toronto. The 14 worst teams in the league had a chance to draft the No. 1 pick. NHL Deputy Commissioner Bill Daly opened an envelope that contained 14 oversize cards, one for each team. The team that had a gold card would have the chance to draft first. Daly revealed them to the cameras slowly, one at a time, from Boston, with a 1% chance of picking first, to Buffalo, with the best chance at 20%. After 11 cards and none gold, the draft was down to three, Edmonton, Arizona and Buffalo. Daly pulled out Edmonton's card, and it was gold. The Oilers would draft Connor McDavid, and the Sabres would pick Eichel.[34]

At first, Sabres GM Tim Murray sounded disappointed by not getting McDavid. "If you can pick 1 or 2, you're going to choose 1. Anytime you can get 1 vs. 2 in any walk of life, you're going to want No. 1. But we came up here with an expectation we'd probably be picking No. 2 and we're going to deal with it. There's no issue there."[35] It was not exactly a ringing endorsement of a player who had 26 goals, 45 assists and 71 points in just 40 games at Boston University. Murray quickly backtracked and said "He's as ready as 99 percent of the 18-year-old kids that have jumped into the National Hockey League. You could say Sidney Crosby was more ready. You could. I'm a scout. I've scouted all my life. But these guys are guys anybody can see are special. It doesn't take me as the GM of the Buffalo Sabres to tell you guys these guys are special."[36] Jack Eichel wasn't in a hurry to publicly commit to playing for the Sabres. "It's hard to talk about playing for a team next year when the draft hasn't happened. A lot of things can happen on draft day. Nothing is set in stone right now, but it would be really nice to play there. There's so much tradition there and it's a great hockey city."[37]

All was forgiven on June 26th, when the NHL prospects gathered in Sunrise, Florida to take part in the NHL Draft. After the Edmonton Oilers selected Connor McDavid, Tim Murray went to the microphone, skipped the speech and simply shouted "Buffalo selects Jack Eichel."[38] Eichel was happy to become a Buffalo Sabre. "It's a great feeling to be selected, especially in an organization like this. There's so much passion and tradition. You look at the Buffalo community and everyone is really into their hockey and knowledgeable…To finally be putting this jersey on, it's a tremendous feeling."[39]

Murry had pulled off a win, and selected one of the top two players in the draft. As of this writing, Eichel has scored 354 game points, 137 goals, 200 assists and 337 total points in his Buffalo Sabres career.[40] The Sabres also named Eichel captain at the beginning of the 2018-19 season. Things could easily have turned out differently. If the Sabres had beaten the Chicago Blackhawks to tie with Arizona, or the team had played better overall, or GM Tim Murray hadn't made certain moves that made it easier for the Sabres to finish in last place, Buffalo wouldn't have drafted Jack Eichel. If the team hadn't, how would the local hockey scene be different?

Matt Sabuda, WBFO sports commentator, feels that it's ironic that the Edmonton Oilers took themselves out of the running for last place by winning a few games at the end of the 2014-15 season. In spite of finishing third in the standings the Oilers got the No. 1 draft pick, Connor McDavid. If the Sabres had won a few more games it's possible that they could have drafted first, and McDavid might have been a Buffalo Sabre while Jack Eichel went to another team. "I think they (the Sabres) were trying to tank. But the irony of the end of that season…teams that were really in the end of the tank were the Sabres, the Coyotes and the Oilers. But the Oilers actually went on a little bit of a hot streak towards the end and played a lot harder than people gave them credit for and racked up a few more wins to get themselves out of that derby…So the balls and the numbers that they were assigned obviously lead them to Connor McDavid. The irony there was that a team that did not go all out to tank at the very end was the team that landed that top prize. So, you almost have to wonder sometimes that there's something to it. Had the Sabres not done that, had the Sabres racked up a few more wins and ended up with that set of ping pong balls instead of the one they did, who knows?"[41]

Tim Graham, former Buffalo News sports reporter and senior writer at The Athletic, likes the idea of tanking in principle, but thinks the Sabres went about it the wrong way. They needed a strong group of supporting players to create a culture of winning, and it was unfair to expect Jack Eichel to miraculously turn the sinking Buffalo Sabres ship around. "I actually liked the tank in principle. The idea of losing to get the best possible player I don't think is a great sin. I know that a lot of people do find it to be an affront to sportsmanship. I did not. But I think they did it the wrong way. They didn't have any cast. They needed more than just Jack Eichel. Especially in hockey, when you're talking about a non-goaltender. One player will never make that huge of a difference to go from being last place in the NHL to Stanley Cup contender."

Sabres GM Tim Murray and newly signed player Jack Eichel at their first press conference, July 1, 2015. Some sports pundits criticized Murray for deliberately tanking to land the No. 2 NHL draft pick. The Buffalo Sabres selected Eichel while the Edmonton Oilers won the draft lottery to choose the No. 1 pick, Connor McDavid. *Photo by AP.*

"The pressure that's been put on Jack Eichel to be the savior is unfair to him, it's not his fault. But they didn't have any supporting cast to speak of. They were selling off the people who could have been the supporting cast in an effort to be as bad as possible so that way they didn't accidentally win games down the homestretch."[42]

Graham also feels, ironically, had the Buffalo Bills not had what became a 17-year long playoff drought, Buffalo sports fans would not have supported the tank as strongly as they did, because they were tired of watching their sports teams lose and were desperate for something, anything to give them a glimmer of hope. A winning Bills team makes tanking for a No. 1 draft pick irrelevant. "It would be interesting to see if the tank would have been such a big deal if the Bills had gone to the playoffs once or twice. I think that the backdrop of the Bills in the 17-year play-off drought, not at that time but it got to 17 years was, we are sick of this. We are going to try the most...desperate thing we can as a solution because nothing else has worked. And had the Bills experienced some sort of joy or the fans I should say experienced some sort of joy along the way...then everybody's a little more tolerant of what's going on with the Sabres."

"I went back and looked at the history of it, too. When the Bills weren't winning the Sabres were, and when the Bills were winning the Sabres weren't. They took their turns. Rarely was there a season when they both stunk. It was usually some source of joy along the way and then they hit this little ball where neither team was doing anything. I think that fans just got desperate for some sort of cure-all and they're still miserable."[43]

Sal Maiorana, author and Rochester Democrat and Chronicle sports reporter, believes that teams don't tank, and Buffalo didn't have a strategy to tank during the 2014-15 season. GMs and coaches won't jeopardize their job security over getting top draft picks. The Sabres finished last because they were the worst team in the NHL, and it wasn't because of effort. "I have a real problem with the word tanking because...as someone who's been 35 years in the business. ...tanking in a professional locker room, is basically akin to committing a cardinal sin. You want to win no matter what. You're not trying to lose so the franchise can get better draft picks and I really believe that the general managers that run these teams, don't want to do that either. They're trying to win too; their jobs are tied to wins and losses."

"I just will not believe that Tim Murray was purposely driving that team into the ground. One of those top two picks they got one just by the fact that they weren't very competitive that year. They had nothing. They had no offense. They were terrible on defense and goaltending wasn't very good. That's a recipe for finishing dead last without the word tanking being used. Who knows? I mean unless he (Murray) was going to come clean and admit that which he'll never do. I've just been around professional sports too long to think that he was purposely trying to lose...How do you look at your veteran players and lay out that type of strategy?... We're going to bring this kid up because we're probably going to have less of a chance to win if we play him four or five games…I just don't think that happens in professional sports."[44]

Sabres forward Jack Eichel celebrates a hat trick goal during the 3rd period against the Ottawa Senators at KeyBank Center in Buffalo, Nov. 16, 2019. *Photo by AP.*

Maiorana also thinks Connor McDavid was the best player in the draft, and it's unfortunate that the Sabres couldn't choose him. "The Sabres didn't need to use the word tanking when they came to that next season when everyone thought they were allegedly tanking. That team lost, they weren't trying to lose, it was just a good thing that in that particular draft with McDavid and Eichel being up, that the Sabres were really awful and they happened to finish where they finished. It was unfortunate that they didn't win the lottery because in my mind…Connor McDavid was the preeminent player in that draft… Jack Eichel was great but he's no Connor McDavid. The Sabres finished last, they should have had him. McDavid was the prize…Eichel is a good player, maybe he'll be a great player someday, but he's not Connor McDavid so it was a shame."[45]

Paul Wieland, author and former Sabres public relations director, is not very enthused about Jack Eichel's performance as a player. Wieland agrees with Maiorana that McDavid was the prize of the draft. Even so, he hasn't helped Edmonton become a hockey dynasty. Good teams need a whole roster of talented players to be competitive. The Las Vegas Golden Knights in their first season are a prime example. "Eichel doesn't impress me much but I watch him all the time and I don't think he knows how to backcheck at all and I don't think he bothers to. I think he's started this year at the end of the year, backcheck at least in the neutral zone. And he wasn't able to try to play around, but he has yet to show me…that he can lead a team to victory."

"McDavid on the other hand…got them (Edmonton) in the playoffs once. They didn't even make them last year either. And he's marvelous. He's a better player than Eichel. So, it isn't always one player, you have to build a team around them these days. I mean look at Las Vegas, how many guys…that started the team would you even know, very few. As a hockey fan even I looked at the roster and I went where do they get these guys? And yet they were a marvelous team to watch, they had wonderful goaltending which was fortunate, you watched it, I watched it. I mean what if they had one more scorer? They might have won the Stanley Cup in their first year. But they ran out of offense little bit."[46]

Chris Ostrander, sportswriter for Two in the Box.com, believes that the Sabres had a strategy to rebuild several years before the 2014-15 season. The Sabres did have a plan to tank. Even if they had not drafted Eichel, the team would still have had several more losing seasons, because the Sabres were in the midst of a lengthy rebuilding process. "Obviously, they had committed to that decision to earnestly rebuild, as funny as it is because they were really outright tanking in those 13-14 and 14-15 years. But they had gone into the idea that we have to rebuild, probably even going back to 2012-13 maybe even 2011-12…if you wanted to peg the start of the rebuild when they traded Paul Gaustad to get themselves an extra first. So, they were already on that path."

"The pipeline at one point probably in 2013-14 looks strong. You would still have the same results, the players that were in the system already in terms of prospects that were developing were already on the track that they were on. They would still reach the end point that they've reached that we're at today in terms of guys not reaching their full potential…This was not a team that was destined for greatness and for whatever reason Tim Murray tore 'em apart, they were going to be bad. So, I always try to keep that in mind …when I discuss the tank just the fact that they were already rebuilding… they still would have been bad in the Sam Reinhart season… Even if they had won that lottery and gotten Aaron Ekblad I don't think he would have made the difference that would have taken them out of the top five in 2017 nor do I think that they would have finished…30th in 2014, if they hadn't been tanking outright."[47]

Ostrander also feels that if the team didn't finish last they wouldn't have drafted Eichel because Arizona was also racing to the bottom. In addition, he agrees with other commentators that Edmonton got a lucky lottery ball bounce that could have turned out differently. "There was a little bit of hypocrisy surrounding it… Had they not been so overt about it like acquiring the two worst statistical goalies during that season, they'd probably miss him (Eichel) just knowing how close it was. In a vacuum if we're just looking at the 2015 season…there was just that year and what they did that season, they'd probably miss him because Arizona was kind of doing the same thing. Then of course Edmonton got the bounce of a lottery ball."[48]

John Krieger, sportswriter for Hockey Central.com, feels that the Sabres were fortunate to draft Jack Eichel. Of course Connor McDavid would also be a great choice, but Eichel is still in the same talent level as McDavid. Without the finish in 30th place after the 2014-15 season, Buffalo might have drafted a player with less ability than either of the first two picks, and this could have slowed the rebuild. "By this time (the tank) I was definitely a lifelong Sabres fan and so this meant a lot to me to get Jack Eichel. If they hadn't tanked to draft Jack, they probably would have ended up with McDavid. That's definitely a joke but we still would have had a top three pick, probably would have ended up with a guy like Dillon Strohm who…hasn't had that much success in the NHL. I think he will be a great player but there's a difference between that kind of player and Jack Eichel who is now our team's captain. So, if we hadn't drafted Jack things would not be where they are. Obviously, we could have ended up with Austin Mathews the year after because we still weren't a good team Jack's rookie year, but I think he was a big boost and we were not as bad as we were the prior year or as bad as we would be without Jack on that team. I couldn't be happier. Obviously both McDavid and Matthews are phenomenal players. Any team would be lucky to have either one of them but Jack is right there in the same conversation. Can't be happier with him. I think he's going to be captain for a long time, hopefully lift up a few Cups as well."[49]

No Sabres tank during the 2014-15 season and no Jack Eichel. The Sabres might have gotten lucky like the Edmonton Oilers and drafted Connor McDavid, the player Tim Murray wanted all along. Or, the franchise may have been so terrible that tanking was unnecessary. If the franchise hadn't finished last in 2015, Jack Eichel could be an Arizona Coyote. If the Sabres had won the lottery in 2016, Austin Matthews might be a Buffalo Sabre. If the Buffalo Bills had played better during the early 21st century, public support for the tank could have been far less and the Sabres might have a stronger group of players, regardless of the draft lottery results. All of these scenarios are possible outcomes. Some sports pundits believe Jack Eichel isn't a prize, and is an overrated hockey player. They question the wisdom of tanking to draft him. Eichel hasn't miraculously turned around the Sabres. No doubt in the 1980s, there were fans who questioned tanking for Mario Lemieux. The Pittsburgh Penguins didn't make the playoffs for five seasons after Lemieux joined the team, and didn't win a Stanley Cup until 1991. The Lemieux tank went against everything sports is supposed to be about, it angered the players and cost the head coach his job. In the end, it helped transform a struggling franchise. Nobody would question the wisdom of that tank today.

CHAPTER 7
What if the NHL Had Disallowed Brett Hull's Goal in Game 6 of the 1999 Stanley Cup Finals?

AT THE END OF THE 1998-99 season, the Buffalo Sabres were on a roll. The team had finished the regular season 37-28-17, with a comfortable 4th place in the NHL's Northeast Division.[1] Buttressed by an outstanding goaltender, Dominik Hasek, who won his third Vezina trophy that year, and led by captain Michael Peca and a crew of talented offensive and defensive players including Miroslav Satan, Alexei Zhitnik, Stu Barnes and Joe Juneau, the Sabres were on a serious winning streak. Buffalo had made it to the Conference Finals the previous year, and the '99 playoffs looked to be another exciting run.[2]

The Sabres had to face the Ottawa Senators in the Eastern Conference Quarter-finals. After beating the Senators 2-1 in Game 1, Buffalo had to play two overtimes against Ottawa to win Game 2 with a 3-2 victory. The Sabres shut out the Senators 3-0 in Game 3. Facing elimination, Ottawa managed to score three goals in Game 4, but it was too little, too late. Buffalo won 4-3, and swept their first-round opponents in four games.[3] The Sabres would face a tougher opponent in the Boston Bruins in the second playoff round, the Conference Semifinals. Buffalo split the first two games in Boston, but when the team came back to Western New York the Sabres took over, winning both games at home to make it a 3-1 series. The Bruins would win a 5-3 victory in Boston to stay alive, but it was only postponing the inevitable. In Game 6 in Marine Midland Arena at home, Buffalo won 3-2 to eliminate the Bruins.[4]

The Eastern Conference Finals would be the Sabres' ultimate test against their longtime rival and nemesis, the Toronto Maple Leafs. Incredibly, this series would be the only time both teams have faced each other in the NHL playoffs. Dominik Hasek was injured in Game 1, so backup goalie Dwayne Roloson had to fill in. If the Leafs thought Hasek was carrying the Sabres they were mistaken. Toronto had a 3-2 lead midway through the game, but Stu Barnes tied the score at the 14:37 mark of the second period. In the third period, Curtis Brown and Geoff Sanderson stepped up for Buffalo to score a goal apiece and contribute to the Sabres' 5-4 victory. The Leafs would have their revenge in Game 2, with Steve Sullivan and Sylvain Cote scoring two goals 18 seconds apart in the first period to give Toronto a 2-0 lead. The Sabres managed to bounce back but by the end of the third period the Leafs held the lead at 4-3. They would widen the score with a Steve Thomas goal with 7:43 remaining to make it 5-3 Toronto. Buffalo would pull their goaltender for an extra attacker but the Leafs got the breakaway and sealed their win with an empty net goal and a 6-3 final score.[5]

The rivals traveled back to Buffalo for Games 3 and 4. Dominik Hasek was back in the net for the Sabres, but the Leafs scored first, with a goal from Toronto forward Yannic Perreault. Buffalo answered back with three goals in the first 7 minutes and 38 seconds of the second period. The Leafs would score another goal, but when Toronto tried to add an extra attacker and even it up, Curtis Brown scored on an empty net to win the game for the Sabres 4-2. Buffalo dominated Game 4 with five goals in two periods. The Leafs would score twice, but it wasn't enough. Dominik Hasek made 31 saves to advance the Sabres to Game 5 with a 3-1 series lead. In Game 5 in Toronto, after a scoreless first period, Steve Sullivan netted one for the Leafs to make it 1-0. After two periods and a few more goals by both teams the game was tied 2-2. Erik Rasmussen broke the tie and scored a Sabres goal at the 11:35 mark of the third. The Leafs desperately tried to stave off elimination and pulled their goaltender, but Dixon Ward broke away and made an empty net goal with 1:02[6] remaining to send the Sabres to the Stanley Cup Finals for the first time since 1975.

What if the NHL Had Disallowed Brett Hull's Goal
in Game 6 of the 1999 Stanley Cup Finals?

Hockey observers were stunned by how fast the underdog Sabres advanced to the finals. This was a team that was in a rebuilding phase that was expected to take years. Even Sabres veteran Rob Ray was surprised by the team's seemingly unstoppable run. "Five or six years ago when we had a team with guys like (Dale) Hawerchuk, (Alexander) Mogilny, (Pat) LaFontaine and (Grant) Fuhr in the net, we said 'Hey, we have a team that can go to the finals and win it.' But we underachieved a lot of the time and never even came close. When they started to rebuild the team, we were thinking, 'This is going to take a long time.' (John) Muckler came in here and brought in a lot of young guys, and I hoped I was going to be around when it happened. But I really didn't think I was going to be around for the time it would take."[7] Sabres broadcaster Rick Jeanneret thought Buffalo fans were more excited about the team's Stanley Cup run than the last time it happened in 1975. "I'm telling you right now, I don't remember this much hype and hullabaloo when the Sabres went to the final with Philadelphia. It was good, but this has everybody attracted. I haven't been pumped like this in years. I've talked to people who don't know one end of the stick from the other who are excited about it."[8]

The Sabres and their fans awaited the results of the Western Conference Finals. The Dallas Stars beat the Colorado Avalanche in Game 7 on June 4th to advance to the Stanley Cup Finals against the Sabres.[9] Game 1 took place in Dallas on June 8th. Brett Hull scored first for the Stars, but in the 3rd period the Sabres finally got on the board with goals from Stu Barnes and Wayne Primeau to make it 2-1 Buffalo. Jere Lehtinen answered back with one minute left to tie the game and force an overtime. In overtime, the Sabres would win the first game of the series with a goal by Jason Wooley. Two days later, after no score in the first period, Michael Peca scored for the Sabres to take the opening lead. Jamie Lagenbrunner answered back for Dallas late in the period to tie the game. In the 3rd period Craig Ludwig made it 2-1 Dallas, but Alexei Zhitnik answered again for the Sabres. However, the Stars took over and scored two more goals to win the game 4-2.[10]

In Game 3, the teams returned to Buffalo. Stu Barnes scored first for the Sabres in the second, but Joe Nieuwendyk tied it for Dallas and scored a second goal in the 3rd period to win it 2-1. Dallas' defense held the Sabres to a franchise record of only 12 shots on goal. Sabres captain Michael Peca was frustrated by the defensive wall the Stars put up. "They can sure make it feel like you've got a plastic bag over your head sometimes. Their team defense is suffocating at times, but we didn't have many second and third efforts. They were one step ahead of us in all areas of the ice."[11]

The Sabres would need to be one step ahead of the Stars in their next meeting, and they were. In Game 4, Geoff Sanderson got a goal in the first period for Buffalo and Jere Lehtinen got one for Dallas to make it a 1-1 game. In the second period Dixon Ward scored an unanswered Buffalo goal at the 7:37 mark. That would be it for the scoring, as the Sabres stayed alive and evened the series two games each. Game 5 in Dallas was a lopsided Stars victory, with Darryl Sydor and Pat Verbeck scoring twice to win the game 2-0 and force the Sabres into a must-win Game 6.[12] The Sabres were confident they could find a way to win and force a Game 7 in Dallas. Jere Lehtinen netted an early goal on Dominik Hasek, and Stu Barnes tied it up in the second period. The game would remain tied for the rest of regulation. It went to overtime, and nobody could score during the first overtime period. Because it was not a regulation game, it went to a second overtime period. Again neither team could score. Incredibly, Game 6 would go into a third overtime. 14 minutes and 51 seconds into the third overtime period, Dallas Stars player Brett Hull shot the puck just outside the crease at Sabres goaltender Dominik Hasek. Hasek stopped the shot, which came out of the crease. Hull then put his left foot in the goal crease and shot the puck past Hasek into the net.[13]

The Dallas Stars erupted onto the ice in celebration. They paraded around the rink with the Stanley Cup congratulating themselves while bitter, heartbroken Sabres fans left the arena on what's normally a happy situation, being out on a warm summer night in Buffalo. Sportswriter J. David Brand was at the game about 15 rows up from the Sabres' net. Brand recalled seeing Hull in the crease but he couldn't see the puck. He remembered fans being crushed after Hull's goal went in the net. Stunned, he watched in disbelief as the Stars players celebrated. Then Brand looked over to see Sabres coach Lindy Ruff slamming the door to his team's bench and yelling. Unable to take any more, he ran out of the arena. Brand could not watch the Dallas Stars skating victory laps in the Sabres' rink.[14]

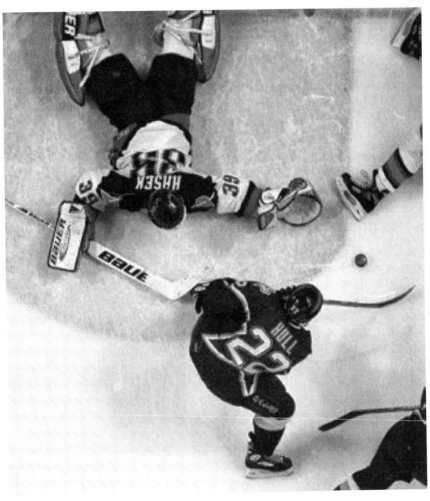

The infamous "No Goal". With one foot in the goal crease, Dallas Stars winger Brett Hull shoots the puck past Buffalo Sabres goaltender Dominik Hasek during Game 6 of the Stanley Cup Finals, June 20, 1999. NHL Commissioner Gary Bettman allowed Hull's goal to stand, even though it violated NHL rules and awarded the Stars the Cup over that goal. *Photo by AP.*

Coach Ruff had a good reason to yell and slam doors. Moments after the game was over, video replay showed that Brett Hull's foot was in the crease during the rebound, after Hasek had blocked his first shot and the puck came out of the crease. At the time, the NHL rules stated that "Unless the puck is in the goal crease area, a player of the attacking side may not enter nor stand in the goal crease. If a player has entered the crease prior to the puck and subsequently the puck should enter the net while such conditions prevail, the apparent goal shall not be allowed."[15] Ruff became livid after league officials refused to review the goal, and NHL Commissioner Gary Bettman refused to listen to Ruff's side of the story. "It was our worst nightmare" Ruff said. "Somebody should have called from upstairs and said, 'This is not a goal.' All I wanted was a review. I wanted Bettman to answer the question of why this wasn't reviewed. He turned his back on me. It was almost as if he knew the goal was tainted. You can't explain the feeling."[16]

What was most galling to the Sabres was that the NHL had disallowed more than 100 goals during the 1998-99 season for violating the foot in the crease rule.[17] Yet, when it came to the Stanley Cup, the league decided to let a goal stand that would have been waved off in many a regular season game that year. To let Brett Hull's goal stand when similar goals had been disallowed was unfair to Buffalo Sabres defenseman Jay McKee. "If there's a guy in the crease before the puck goes in there, the goal doesn't count. It has happened all season long. We're not whining; that's the rule. To have it end that way is devastating for us."[18] McKee felt that if the Stars were going to beat the Sabres, at least they could have done it with a real goal.[19] Bryan Lewis, the NHL's supervisor of officiating, tried to justify the goal by saying that Brett Hull had continuous possession of the puck, so therefore the goal was legal. Under normal circumstances, a video review judge in the press box would make certain that the goal was legal. Lewis claimed the video review judge did this, however, anytime a play was under review, the public-address announcer would tell the fans that it was under review. The announcer never made that call, which made the Sabres feel that the goal was never reviewed, in spite of Lewis' claim.[20]

What if the NHL Had Disallowed Brett Hull's Goal in Game 6 of the 1999 Stanley Cup Finals?

Even some of the Dallas Stars admitted the goal was questionable. "I saw it, and it looked like he did (put his foot in the crease)" center Mike Modano said. "But what can you do, drag us back out there and play?"[21] That's exactly what Sabres goaltender Dominik Hasek thought they should have done. Sports Illustrated writer Michael Farber wrote that Hasek saw the video replay and got ready to get back in the net because he assumed Hull's goal wasn't legitimate. "When Hasek saw the replay in the dressing room, he got ready to tug his sweater back on because he assumed the game would start again. "They told me 'Dom, it's over'" Hasek said, and I said 'But it's not a goal.'"[22]

Sabres captain Michael Peca, like Lindy Ruff, tried to speak to Gary Bettman, but Bettman would not acknowledge him. "I tried to be nice" Peca said. "I said, Gary, the guy's foot was in the crease. But he turned and walked away. Wouldn't listen."[23] Bettman denied that Peca spoke to him, but he told Sports Illustrated that "Mr. Ruff's conduct was out of control and inappropriate. I'm not sure he was in any condition to have a conversation."[24] Bettman's conduct was biased, to say the least. The NHL refused to overturn Brett Hull's goal, and the league awarded the Dallas Stars the Stanley Cup trophy because of it. Dominik Hasek was bitter about how the Sabres' Stanley Cup run ended. "There is no doubt that the goal left a bad taste in everyone's mouth as we headed into the offseason. After everything we accomplished and how well we played during our playoff run, it was a shame it had to end this way."[25] Joe Juneau believed the league didn't want to acknowledge their mistake, and make the Stars put their champagne back in its buckets. "The goal was not a legal goal. I think because it was a goal that gave them the Stanley Cup, everybody jumped on the ice and they were afraid to make the call."[26]

If the NHL had been willing to review the goal, and NHL Commissioner Gary Bettman was more open to listening to the Sabres' point of view, which is admittedly a stretch, how would Game 6 have ended? Could the Sabres have come back on the ice and won the game, forced a Game 7 in Dallas, and possibly won the Stanley Cup?

Paul Wieland, author and former Sabres public relations director, believes that if the NHL had disallowed Brett Hull's goal and the teams kept playing, the Sabres could have won Game 6 and possibly the Cup. Officials make bad calls all the time, and the on-ice officials should have reviewed the goal. Buffalo's 1999 team was at the top of their game, with a superb offense and defense, plus goaltender Dominik Hasek. They could have beaten Dallas in Game 6 and ultimately, won the Stanley Cup. "Sure (the Sabres could have won). It was a competitive series. It could have turned on that, it could turn back and Buffalo could have…legitimately won the game because they were in the series to that point and so it's odd because when an official misses a call you sort of run with that in sports. Umpires (miss) ball strikes, they screw it up all the time. But that's a hard call to make with video replays. You couldn't if they're allowed to be used and they are used in the NHL. (Had it been used) probably that goal would have not counted. So, if Buffalo had protested and asked for a video replay they probably would have shown he (Brett Hull) was in the crease. However, it wasn't that way. It's wonderful to think about the Sabres winning a Stanley Cup and with Dominik Hasek and all that. But you know, what if."[27]

Wieland added that Dominik Hasek was the backup goalie from the Chicago Blackhawks, and acquiring him was one the Sabres' fortunate moves. In 2001, the Sabres traded Hasek to the Detroit Red Wings, where he finally won a Stanley Cup. With his level of talent, there's no reason he couldn't have gotten a Cup for Buffalo. "Hasek was a throw-in in the deal when they (the Sabres) got him. He was the second-stringer in Chicago and he was wacky; if you ever met him and talked to him he's a little wacky. I remember talking to him and having dinner with him one night right after he was traded to Buffalo. It was myself and another guy in Long Island and he was kind of an odd duck, but boy he could play…look he went to Detroit and won a Stanley Cup for them. So just one foot in the crease might have been the difference. I'll agree that sure it could have happened the other way. They would have been able to call that play as a violation of the rules."[28]

Tim Graham, former Buffalo News sports reporter and senior writer at The

Athletic, disagrees with Wieland that the Sabres could have won the Cup if the league had disallowed Brett Hull's foot in the crease goal. The Stars would have had home ice advantage going back to Dallas for Game 7, if the Sabres had forced it. However, he agrees with Wieland and the majority of Sabres fans that it was unfair to award Dallas the Stanley Cup over that disputed goal. "Chances are the Stars still win the Stanley Cup...The Stars still have a 50/50 chance of winning that game and then the series returns to Dallas for Game 7. So, a lot of people view that like they view Norwood's field goal (in Super Bowl XXV). If Norwood makes the kick the Bills win the Super Bowl. If the goal is disallowed the Sabres win the Cup. I think that there are a lot of fans out there who just assume that had the NHL flipped the script on that, then the Sabres have their Cup but so much still had to happen."

"There are a lot of narratives that you get in your mind as a sports fan of that one thing being a cause. So yeah, it was clearly a botched call. Foot was in the crease should have been disallowed. The celebration had gone on too long on the ice. I don't have this as inside knowledge but as an outsider it clearly was, we can't put the genie back in the bottle, the toothpaste back in the tube, whatever metaphor you want to use. The Stars are already skating around with the Cup. We can't take it from them and then start the game back up. So, I would say the Stars still probably win the Cup. Because they had the advantage going back home. But it was unfairly won, that's for sure."[29]

Graham also believes that the National Hockey League, in his opinion, is light years behind the NFL in how it runs its operations. The "No Goal" fiasco and the next day rule change to make a player's foot in the crease legal is a prime example. "The NHL has a history of making it up as it goes. It's such a poorly run league. The NFL has so many flaws, but compared to the NHL it is perfect. The NHL just puts it to shame in terms of mismanagement. I do like that the way the NHL will radically change its rules just to try new things like going back to allow two line passes, no touch offsides, 3 on 3 overtime. I like the shootout. So, I like that the

NHL at least tries things but...it is such a Neanderthal league. It's progressive on one hand but still stuck in the past. And so much seems to be clandestine. They decided to make up these rules and not tell anybody about them like the memo that supposedly had gone out."[30]

Chris Ostrander, sportswriter for Two in the Box.com, thinks that the game could have turned on a missed shot, if James Patrick had scored a goal earlier in the game, instead of missing the net. Had that happened, Game 6 wouldn't have gone into overtime. "You know it's funny because James Patrick hits the cross bar from two shifts before that or whatever it was. And I think back to the 2010 (Olympic) gold medal game and Zach Parise at the cross bar two shifts before Crosby's goal in OT. So, (without that chance) I don't think they win the Cup. You talk to (Sabres) hockey players and they say we got robbed. And it should have been our Cup. But I don't know if they win that game."[31]

Ostrander also believes the Dallas Stars were the better team, and Dominik Hasek carried the Sabres into the Stanley Cup Finals. Even if the NHL had disallowed Brett Hull's goal, it was only postponing the inevitable. The 1999 Sabres could not have won four games against the Stars, and the Dallas team would have eventually prevailed, if not in Game 6 then definitely in Game 7. "The Stars were the better team. They were. They had more guns. They were going to outscore the Sabres eventually. It was just a matter of time until... they just overwhelmed Hasek. So, I don't think they would have won the Cup. Maybe they win the game because they had found their luck in the games prior to that a number of times. So, in terms of winning that game...it was certainly possible but I don't think they win the Cup. I know there's been a couple Stars players if I'm not mistaken have come out and said we were dead tired. I don't think we would have beaten them in a Game 7, but back on home ice (Dallas), having to travel again...they (the Sabres) just kept kicking that can down the road. That was not an offensive team, the Sabres. That was a team built around Dominik Hasek and they were going to try to limit as many shots as they could. At the end of the day it was all about Hasek bailing them out. So, I don't think they win the Cup, I really don't."[32]

What if the NHL Had Disallowed Brett Hull's Goal
in Game 6 of the 1999 Stanley Cup Finals?

Matt Sabuda, WBFO sports commentator, feels that the Sabres had a chance to beat the Stars. Overall the Stars were the better team, and much of Buffalo's Stanley Cup run was built around Dominik Hasek's goaltending ability. However, if the Brett Hull goal wasn't a factor, the Sabres could have won Game 6, and Game 7s are often unpredictable. "If you ran through the scenarios…generally the Sabres were pretty overmatched as a team with the exception of having the greatest goalie in the world backing them up where if that goal was disallowed, I still feel like it would have been 50-50 at best that they ended up winning that game. But you never know. Hey I'll take one lucky shot. I remember the very first game of that series was pretty much won in overtime on exactly that scenario. I think it was a James Patrick slap shot that put the Sabres up one nothing in the Cup Finals in overtime. So, all it would have taken was one to get to a Game 7 and in Game 7 anything can happen."[33]

Author Ross Brewitt pointed out that if the Sabres had played better during the finals, the Cup would not have come down to Brett Hull's goal in Game 6. In addition, it was useless to argue against the referees, because they weren't about to overturn the call. "I think the thing was the Sabres needed to score a couple of more times. Your job as a team is to score goals. If the other team scores more goals than you, then obviously, they win. If they had scored six goals in the first period they wouldn't have been worried about it. Maybe it was wrong, and maybe it was a bad call by a referee. But regardless if they had won, or it was a fair win or not, the call was made. The game was over. Maybe it was an error on the referee's time. But that happens."[34]

John Krieger, sportswriter for Hockey Central.com, didn't remember watching the game, but from people he spoke with, Sabres fans at the time expected they would win the Stanley Cup. He agreed with other observers that the Dallas Stars were the better team, and the Sabres had a great goaltender in Hasek. If the Sabres had won the Cup, Hasek would not have insisted on being traded to the Detroit Red Wings, where he was part of a Stanley Cup championship team. Hasek would have ended his career as a Sabres goalie, and it's possible he could have lifted more than one Cup over his head. "I'll start with the fact that I was 3 years old when this happened. So, I don't personally really have a memory of this. I did talk to my father about it and he kind of jokingly said that if that goal hadn't been allowed… he would probably still be wearing the championship gear today. So, I think a lot of Sabres fans back then probably thought we were going to win. From a nonbiased standpoint, Dallas was the one seed I believe. I believe Buffalo was the seventh seed. So, we might not have been favored. I do think Hasek was a big part of that team's success that year, obviously couldn't have done it without him. If we had won, Hasek played two more years after that and then he was just kind of done. He wanted to try to go win a Cup and he didn't think this team that we had could do it. Had we won the Cup that year maybe Hasek sticks out the last however many years of his career. He retires as a Sabre, maybe another Cup or two. It's hard to say."[35]

If league officials had disallowed Brett Hull's goal, the Sabres could have won Game 6 and forced a Game 7. It's possible that the Dallas Stars were the better team, although the Stars were made up of older players who might have collapsed in a Game 7, where the Sabres' youth and endurance could have made the difference. Then again, the Stars showed that they had an offensive and defensive depth during the series, and the Sabres seemed to struggle to close out too many must-win games. Without a No Goal, Dominik Hasek would have remained a Buffalo Sabre, and with no controversial missed call to demoralize the team, Buffalo might have won a Stanley Cup, if not that year, maybe in the next two or three. Certainly the 1999 team was Cup worthy, and no Buffalo roster since that time has made it to the finals. We'll never know, but one thing is for sure. Sabres fans long to return to the Stanley Cup Finals someday, and when they do, they hope this time the outcome won't be in doubt.

CHAPTER 8
What if the Vancouver Canucks Had Picked Gilbert Perreault in the 1970 NHL Draft?

In the 1960s, the National Hockey League decided to expand. Since World War II, the NHL's fan base had their choice of six teams, the Boston Bruins, Chicago Black Hawks, Detroit Red Wings, Montreal Canadiens, New York Rangers and Toronto Maple Leafs. In order for interest in hockey to grow, the league needed more teams. More teams also meant more money for the league, because each owner that wanted an NHL franchise had to pay a franchise fee that fattened the league's coffers. In 1967, the NHL decided on a new round of expansion cities, six new teams to double the NHL's size. The Oakland Seals, Los Angeles Kings, Minnesota North Stars, Philadelphia Flyers, Pittsburgh Penguins and St. Louis Blues,[1] would make hockey a more geographically broad, popular and hopefully lucrative sport.

Many Canadians were outraged because not one of the new expansion teams was in Canada. Canadians had invented hockey, after all, and the NHL had always included Canadian franchises. Hockey enthusiasts in Vancouver, Canada's major West Coast metropolis, didn't like being left out of the 1967 expansion round. Hockey fans in Buffalo, a sports-crazy Great Lakes town on the Canadian border, couldn't understand why the league had bypassed their city, either. Eventually, the NHL relented. When the league decided to add two more teams in 1970, the two new franchises would be the Vancouver Canucks and the Buffalo Sabres. And in homage to the city where the sport was first played, the NHL would hold both its Expansion and Amateur Drafts at the Queen Elizabeth Hotel in Montreal, Quebec.[2]

The first day of the draft, the Expansion Draft, the Canucks and Sabres managers and coaches wrangled over who would draft a group of cast off players the

The Fairmont Queen Elizabeth Hotel in Montreal, Quebec, Canada in 2017. Built by the Canadian National RY and opened in 1958, the Queen Elizabeth hosted the NHL Expansion and Amateur Drafts in 1970. The Buffalo Sabres and Vancouver Canucks both competed for the No. 1 draft pick, Gilbert Perreault. Thanks to a lucky spin of the wheel, the Sabres chose Perreault, who put the new franchise on a solid footing. *Photo by Meunierd.*

rest of the NHL teams didn't want. Most of these guys were veterans, counting the days until retirement, not the kind of talent new franchises that want to make an impression build their team around. The real action was the Amateur Draft the next day. These young talents, the best juniors in Canada, were what the staff of both new expansion teams eagerly coveted. The first pick available was Gilbert Perreault, from the Montreal Junior Canadiens. Perreault was a smooth, strong and fast center, a franchise player leagues above the rest, or so most observers believed. Someone in the NHL thought it would be a good idea to use a spinning carnival wheel to make the draft selections. Vancouver got the numbers 1 through 9, Buffalo would get 10 through 18. Clarence Campbell, the NHL's president, a prim and proper lawyer who had been at the Nuremburg War Crimes trials after World War II, oversaw the lottery and announced the numbers.[3]

Campbell spun the wheel, and a ballroom full of nervous, tense and excited GMs, coaches and supporting staff from both teams waited for it to stop. Paul Wieland, who had joined the Sabres a few months earlier as their new public relations director, remembered what happened next. "When Campbell spun the wheel...it came up 1 over 1 which is actually 11 but at first the 1 was on top, so all the Vancouver people thought they had the number. But all of a sudden everybody said hey wait a minute that's 11, and that was Buffalo's number."[4] Ross Brewitt, author of A Spin of the Wheel: Birth of the Buffalo Sabres, was also in the ballroom that day. After Campbell had called out 1, "(Sabres coach/GM) Punch Imlach pointed out that the number was not what they called. But when they stopped and somebody...the PA guy or somebody like that said 1...half the room went oh! and the other half went yeah! But anyway, a couple people sitting a little further back that could see it a little better pointed out that it was wrong, and that the number that they had called...was not correct. And everybody had seen it and so it wasn't hurting any argument about it. Then it switched from Vancouver to the Sabres."[5] Campbell was forced to announce "Correction, the number is 11."[6] A table full of Sabres personnel roared their approval. They had picked the No. 1 player in the draft, by the luck of the spin.

Brewitt pointed out that at first, not everybody in the Sabres organization thought they were getting the best draft pick. "You've got to realize at the time, Dale Tallon was the other guy that they were (drafting). Everybody there was two camps about who was going to get drafted first, there was one camp for each guy... Dale's value was that he was both a defenseman and a center and he could play both. He proved it in junior. And you know one didn't hurt the other but the way that came out it wasn't until a long time later that they realized that Perreault was the prize of the draft. Going into the draft it was thought that they were even up. And it depended whether you needed a defenseman that could also play the wing or center or did you want a guy that just simply was a fast skater from the Quebec league? Which you know didn't have the heavy going that the other two junior leagues had."

"That was their concern; there was some concern but it was never Imlach's. Imlach wanted the best player and the best player was Perreault. We're talking now after the fact, this was before the fact and a lot of people thought that maybe they should have gone for Tallon because he could play either defense or center. But when it was the first game that the Sabres played at home (which was the 16th of October) ... people were just wowed by Perreault. He was an instant hit in Buffa-lo."[7]

The Sabres had picked a star player, and they would need him because during those first few months, the Sabres only won seven games. Things got better in January, when the team won six victories. The Sabres would slump again in February, before going on a 15-game winning streak that gave Buffalo a sixth-place finish in the eight team Eastern Division. The Sabres ended the 1970-71 season 24-39-15, ahead of Vancouver, Detroit, Pittsburgh and California. Gilbert Perreault had scored 38 goals to set an NHL rookie scoring record.[8] The spin of the wheel was fortunate indeed.

Buffalo Sabres center Gilbert Perreault flies up the ice in a game against the Washington Capitals (undated). In his career with the Sabres, Perreault holds the franchise record for the most games with 1,191 and scored 512 goals, had 814 assists and 1,326 points. *Photo courtesy of Buffalo Courier Express, Buffalo State College, Archives and Collections.*

Perreault had an amazing first season. The only problem from the Sabres' point of view was, the team didn't have any players on offense who could match his speed. GM Imlach spent the 1971 Amateur Draft trying to find a sniper who could take some of the scoring burden off Perreault. The Sabres had the fifth-round pick, which meant Imlach wouldn't be able to draft Guy LaFleur, the No. 1 pick, who went to the Montreal Canadiens. Detroit took Marcel Dionne, and the Sabres got lucky again because the third choice should have been left winger Rick Martin. As a member of the Junior Canadiens, Martin had scored 71 goals the previous year, but strangely, the Canucks chose his teammate Jocelyn Geuvremont, and the St. Louis Blues went with Gene Carr. Once again Imlach was lucky, and the Sabres picked Martin. Martin had also been Perreault's teammate on the Junior Canadiens, and unlike many French-Canadian prospects, Martin didn't insist on playing for the NHL Canadiens. "I didn't care where I played. A lot of guys wanted to play for Montreal, but I didn't care. I just wanted to be drafted, and I knew I'd have a better chance of making it with an expansion team."[9]

Rick Martin was an instant success, but some of the veterans the team had picked up weren't as productive. Punch Imlach traded Eddie Shack to the Pittsburgh Penguins on March 4th for right winger Rene Robert. The Robert edition helped the team, but the Sabres still finished their second season 12 points behind their first one, 16-43-19, but still ahead of Vancouver (20-50-8). The young players that Imlach was drafting wanted to showcase their skills on the ice. This was important for a new franchise like the Sabres. Sabres player Jim Lorentz remembered that "We had a group of guys who really wanted to prove that we were legitimate NHL players. When you're young, you need that confidence because you don't know if you're good enough to play in the league. That's one of the things we started to find out (at the end of the 1972 season) that a lot of us could develop into pretty good NHL players."[10]

The Sabres were more than pretty good the following season, 1972-73. The team ended that year with a playoff run for the first time in franchise history, after a winning record of 37-27-14.[11] A lot of those wins came courtesy of the French Connection, the high-scoring French-Canadian trio of Gilbert Perreault, Rene Robert and Rick Martin. Hall of Fame New York Islanders defenseman Denis Potvin recalled that his team always dreaded playing the Sabres because they'd have to compete against Perreault and his two wingers. "It was unbelievable because they complemented each other so well. Having Gilbert down the middle created a lot of scoring opportunities for them, and he attracted so much attention. And no line in hockey, I don't think, ever had as many finishers, guys who can finish the play. That's the key to the game. There's a lot of good hockey players who can go up and down and shoot the puck, but there's a natural talent to finishing that you just can't teach. And you had all three of them who could finish a play on you, and that's what was so scary."[12]

The Sabres battled their way into the playoffs, but lost to the Montreal Canadiens in six games. The next season, 1973-74, would be tough for Sabres fans to take. After winning six of their first nine games, Gilbert Perreault suffered a broken leg and missed eight weeks. On top of that blow Sabres goaltender Roger Crozier would be out the rest of the season after he developed pancreatitis. A third tragedy happened when, on February 20, 1974, veteran defenseman Tim Horton decided to drive back to Buffalo by himself after a Sabres game in Toronto against the Leafs. After consuming pain killers and alcohol, Horton crashed his car into a guardrail on the Queen Elizabeth Way, and died. The three hits were too much for the team to overcome, and the Sabres finished in fifth place with a record of 32-34-12, and missed the playoffs.[13]

The 1974-75 season would be the French Connection's zenith. Rene Robert, Gilbert Perreault and Rick Martin finished with the top ten in scoring. The Sabres scored a total of 354 goals that year, and ended the season in first place with a 49-16-15 record.[14] The Sabres came charging out of the playoff gate, and eliminated the Chicago Black Hawks in five games. The team faced the Montreal Canadiens in the Semifinals. Buffalo took a 2-0 series lead before Montreal tied the series

2-2. Game 5 in Buffalo was a must-win for the Sabres, and the French Connection would make the difference. Rene Robert scored an overtime goal to win the game for the Sabres 5-4. Game 6 in Montreal was another Sabres win, as the team scored 4 goals to 3 and went to the Stanley Cup Finals in their fifth season as a franchise. The Sabres would face the defending champion Philadelphia Flyers.[15]

The Blue and Gold lost the first two games in the Broad Street Bullies' rink. In Game 3 at the Aud, Rene Robert would be the overtime hero again when he scored on Flyers' goaltender Bernie Parent with a 5-4 victory. Game 4 was another Sabres win, with the team getting a 4-2 win. Unfortunately, the Flyers won the next two and dashed Buffalo's Stanley Cup hopes. The Sabres made it to the playoffs the rest of the 1970s and well into the 1980s. However, in late 1978 the owners fired GM Punch Imlach and brought in a new combined coach and GM from the Montreal Canadiens, Scotty Bowman. Bowman broke up the French Connection by trading Rene Robert to the Colorado Rockies for defenseman John Van Boxmeer. It was the end of an era. On March 11th 1981, Bowman traded Rick Martin to the L.A. Kings in exchange for draft picks.[16]

Gilbert Perreault continued to play for the Sabres, and he continued to score goals.[17] However, as he approached his mid-30s and the team kept struggling, Perreault reluctantly decided it was time to retire. He held a press conference at Buffalo's Memorial Auditorium in June 1986. Perreault told reporters that "It was a tough decision to make, but there's a time for everything, and today's the day."[18] In spite of his opening statement, Perreault sounded like he had second thoughts at the end of the press conference. He added that "Right now, I don't feel like playing hockey too much, but once September comes, you never know. Sometimes with the right offer and everything, you might change your mind."[19] Coach/GM Scotty Bowman talked him into playing one more season with a one year contract. Yet, after the Sabres struggled to find their bearings and suffered a season opening 4-13-3, Perreault realized his first instinct was right. "If the team had been doing good, maybe things would have been different" he said at his final retirement speech. "But after the start we had, I decided I had enough and it was time to make a change. You need a certain feeling, a special eagerness to want to practice and want to play the game. I had lost that. I just couldn't find it this season."[20]

Perreault thought the Sabres would give him a position in the hockey department. But when management offered him a job as public relations ambassador for the team, he refused. Perreault stayed away from the Sabres until 1990, when he and the owners patched things up. On October 17, 1990, Gilbert Perreault returned to the Aud for a ceremony to retire his No. 11 Jersey. The sellout crowd gave him a three-minute standing ovation. Sabres owner Seymour Knox III presented the hockey legend with a silver stick, and said "There is no player who has meant more to his team than the man we honor tonight."[21]

That wasn't the end of Perreault's relationship with the Buffalo Sabres. More than 20 years later, on February 22, 2011, Terry Pegula held a press conference at HSBC Arena to announce his purchase of the Sabres. Gilbert Perreault, Rene Robert and Rick Martin all came and sat near the new owner. When Pegula caught a glimpse of Perreault, he became choked up. "I'm going to try not look this way too much because of some of the old faces"[22] he managed to say. Pegula added "Where's Perreault? You're my hero."[23] Pegula decided to immortalize the French Connection and he hired sculptor Jerry McKenna to create a bronze statue of Rene Robert, Gilbert Perreault and Rick Martin, based on a photo of the trio taken at a playoff game against the Philadelphia Flyers in April 1975 where each player scored a goal. On October 12, 2012, Terry and Kim Pegula dedicated the statue at the KeyBank Center Plaza. Rene Robert and Gilbert Perreault were there for the honor. Sadly, Rick Martin had passed away in March of 2011. Perreault told the assembled audience that their goal was to put a great show on the ice for Sabres fans. He added that the French Connection was something special and they had some great years playing together. The statue was a great honor and it was a very special night.[24]

Gilbert Perreault was the franchise leader with 512 goals, 814 assists and 1,326 points in his 17 seasons as a Buffalo Sabre. The second player that was available in the 1970 draft, Dale Tallon, lasted three seasons with the Vancouver Canucks before they traded him to the Chicago Black Hawks. Tallon would eventually play 10 seasons in the NHL and score a total of 98 goals and 336 points.[25] It's clear that, in hindsight, the Sabres were lucky the wheel landed on 11 and not 1. But what if it hadn't? What if, in that smoke-filled ballroom at the Queen Elizabeth Hotel in Montreal in June of 1970, the numbers on the wheel had favored the Vancouver Canucks, and they had drafted Gilbert Perreault? How would the future of Buffalo Sabres hockey have turned out?

Paul Wieland, author and former Sabres public relations director, feels that Perreault made the franchise in the Sabres' early days when Buffalo had a young expansion team that needed to make an impression. He also feels that Perreault was the key to the Sabres making it to the 1975 Stanley Cup Finals. Dale Tallon would not have gotten the Sabres anywhere close to a Stanley Cup run. "Gilbert was best and he helped make the franchise because he was worth the price of admission because to watch him, he stick handled and handled the puck as smoothly as anybody you've ever seen. He was big and strong and even when guys hit him he could fight them off and continue his play. He was not selfish, he was a great goal scorer but he set up his teammates, his linemates as much as he set up himself. I don't know if they would have been half as good as they were, they might have been pretty good. But Perreault was the key player to get to the finals. He (Tallon) turned out to have a decent NHL career but…he didn't leave Vancouver anyplace, let's put it that way. Vancouver did nothing at least certainly by '75. They came in the league the same time and they didn't get anyplace until…the late '80s when they had a couple of good teams. Roger Neilson was coaching there one year but… Perreault was still playing. But that was later on."[26]

Wieland also noted that if Sabres goaltender Roger Crozier hadn't developed pancreatitis, he might have made more of a difference during the 1975 Stanley Cup Finals against the Philadelphia Flyers. Wieland believes goaltending was a major factor in that series, and having Roger Cozier in the net for the Sabres instead of Gerry Desjardins could have changed the final outcome. "Now the '75 team, of course. What if Roger Crozier would have been healthy instead of having pancreatitis? He was a pretty sick guy. He couldn't play way back then, he hardly ever practiced. And I know that because I was a practice goalie then and went on the ice in his place for a couple years. He hardly ever practiced because he had pancreatitis although ironically that's not what killed him. So, he was sick and if he could have played in the finals, he played one game near the end of them against Philly. But if he could play all the way I think it was goaltending that won the finals. Bernie Parent for the Flyers was significantly better than Gerry Desjardins for Buffalo. So that's the other what-if, what if Roger Crozier had been healthy, just on that."[27]

Sal Maiorana, author and Rochester Democrat and Chronicle sports reporter, believes Gilbert Perreault was a talent that the Buffalo Sabres were enormously fortunate to land. He was a player that the Sabres needed to draft. He put the franchise in the right direction from the very beginning, and in contrast to the Vancouver Canucks, who struggled throughout the 1970s, the Sabres made the playoffs consistently into the '80s. Perreault's talent was an important factor in the team's success in the early years. "I think all of Buffalo would cry (if the Canucks drafted Perreault) because just like the Eichel-McDavid draft there was no doubt that Gilbert Perreault was the No. 1 pick. I mean it wasn't even close that year. He was far and away best player in that draft. You look at the two franchises and the way they started in the NHL, the Sabres were in the playoffs within three years. I'm not even sure when the Canucks finally got to the playoffs but they were a terrible team pretty much throughout the entire decade of the '70s."[28]

Maiorana also feels that Perreault, along with Jim Kelly and O.J. Simpson, are the best pro athletes to ever play in Buffalo. When Perreault became injured in the 1973-74 season the Sabres missed the playoffs. Having Gilbert Perreault on the team was crucial to the Sabres' winning record and fan support. Vancouver played second fiddle to the Sabres, and the situation would have been reversed without

Perreault's skill. "The Sabres were in the playoff series their third year, they missed the 4th year because Perreault broke his leg and missed too much of the year. They were in the postseason well into the '80s, they made the playoffs 12 or 13 years in a row after '74 so Gilbert Perreault, was I think, without question one of the three most important athletes in Buffalo sports history. (They) were in that order Gilbert Perreault, Jim Kelly and O.J. Simpson. O.J. Simson, say what you want about him. He was one of the greatest talents who ever played professional football in Buffalo. Those are the three for me. Gilbert Perreault for me, with his coming to the Sabres we had the franchise on a proper course from day one. They took their lumps the first two years. I wrote a book about the '72-'73 team. The first team that made the playoffs and Perreault was the key to the whole thing, not even a doubt. Dale Tallon who ended up going No. 2 to Vancouver, Dale Tallon being the first player in franchise history, we shudder to even think how it would have gone for the Sabres at least that first five, six or seven years. Perreault was a dynamic superstar waiting to happen."[29]

Chris Ostrander, sportswriter for Two in the Box.com, agrees with other commentators that without Gilbert Perreault, the Sabres never would have made it to the 1975 Stanley Cup Finals. In addition, without Perreault's dynamic offensive talent, the Sabres would have become a team focused on defense and goaltending, because there would be no French Connection to score consistently on offense. "Obviously, the French Connection would not exist as we know it today. I would say definitively the Sabres would not have been a Cup Finalist in '75. I think that's probably the one definite conclusion you can draw from Perreault's impact on the franchise...They would not be the team that they were early on. I don't know if there would been a long-term impact on the franchise or not. It's kind of hard to say in terms of him being just an iconic cornerstone talent. That's not to take away from the player Dale Tallon was because he was a good player, he was a very good player for the Canucks. I don't think that Dale Tallon becomes a brilliant perennial...candidate playing in Buffalo or anything like that. But it would have been a different team for sure. We'd probably be more obsessed with goaltending and defense than we are now just because we wouldn't have had (Perreault). At least we had Perreault as kind of the first Sabre. One of the very first Sabres is just such a dynamic offensive player. If he wasn't here we'd probably even have less appreciation for big offensive talent."[30]

Bronze statue of Buffalo Sabres players Gilbert Perreault, Rene Robert and Rick Martin in KeyBank Center Plaza, home of the Sabres. Known as the "French Connection" this offensive line was one of the highest scoring in Sabres history. The statue is based on a photo of the trio taken during an April 1975 playoff victory over the Montreal Canadiens. *Photo by Jeff Dahlberg.*

Matt Sabuda, WBFO sports commentator, agrees with Weiland, Ostrander and Maiorana, that without Perreault, there would have been no French Connection, no '75 Stanley Cup run and no way the Sabres would have been a consistently early offensive team. He also feels there were parallels between Gilbert Perreault and Connor McDavid. "I don't think we would have had the excitement of the French Connection certainly before my time. (Dale Tallon) certainly wasn't a guy in the category of Gilbert Perreault. A lot of people looked at Perreault almost from what I understood the way people look at Connor McDavid when he came into this draft. It wasn't really even a one in one A, it was a one in off distant two. I'd have a hard time seeing how (they made the '75 Stanley Cup Finals)."[31]

John Krieger, sportswriter for Hockey Central.com, believes that the Buffalo Sabres would not have been a viable long-term franchise past the 1970s without Perreault's talent and skill. There are parallels between the 1970-71 Sabres and the 2017-18 Las Vegas Golden Knights. New expansion teams need great players to excite their fan bases, especially when a franchise is establishing itself. Getting Perreault in the draft was exactly what the Sabres needed. "The team probably wouldn't have survived the '70s…that's my personal opinion. You look at how the league is…nowadays you look at what Vegas did last year they had a phenomenal start to the franchise, went to the Cup in their first year. And I think that was much needed to really establish a fan base, a strong fan base. Having that kind of player to start your franchise with, that's just huge."[32]

Krieger also feels that having a player like Perreault attracted other gifted players to the Sabres, because talent attracts other talent. "Getting Perreault, that was our trip to the finals in our first year…And I think he was enough to really show our city that we've got a good hockey team, maybe not yet but we've got this guy at least. And having a player like Perreault, you get other players coming in and playing with them."[33]

With no Gilbert Perreault, there may not have been a 1975 Stanley Cup run, or even a Buffalo Sabres franchise today. There would have been no French Connection, and no statues of the fast-moving, high-scoring trio in downtown Buffalo. Without an exciting talent like Perreault, a young Penn State graduate named Terry Pegula wouldn't have become a die-hard Buffalo Sabres fan, and certainly wouldn't have bought the team from Tom Golisano in 2011. So much depended on one spin of the wheel.

CHAPTER 9
What if Buffalo Had a Major League Baseball Team?

BUFFALO, NY HAS LONG BEEN home to the NFL's Buffalo Bills and the NHL's Buffalo Sabres. Many sports fans wonder why Buffalo never landed a major league baseball franchise. In fact, Buffalo's baseball backers made several attempts to secure a major league team in the late 1800s and early 1900s. In 1879, the Buffalo Bisons began playing as part of the National League. The team finished 3rd place out of 10th that year, and they had several solid winning seasons over the next seven years. The Bisons even had two future Hall of Famers in their roster.[1] Overflow crowds came out to watch them play,[2] however the following season the club finished in 7th place and the Bisons were in a precarious financial situation. With an infusion of new capital, the franchise was able to continue. The team's owners hired Jim O'Rourke as both manager and center fielder. First baseman Dan Brouthers joined Jim White, Jack Rowe and Hardy Richardson. The foursome were powerful hitters, and they earned the nickname "The Big Four." The Bisons finished 3rd for the second time in three years in 1881, and pitcher Jim Galvin won 29 games. Brouthers batted .319 and hit eight home runs, White hit .310, Rowe .333, and Richardson had a .291 batting average. Manager O'Rourke managed to get to .300 that season, too.[3] The Bisons were on a hot streak.

The following season, the Bisons tied for 3rd place, but were inexplicably plagued by poor attendance. The next year, they would slide into 5th place. 1884 would be the Buffalo Bisons' best season, with pitcher Jim Galvin winning 46 games and the team getting to 3rd place again. Even so, there were ominous developments. Talented manager Jim O'Rourke left the club and went to New York for the 1885 season. Pitcher Jim Galvin collided with Chicago's Cap Anson on June 19th, and it affected his performance. The Bisons sold his contract to Pittsburgh in mid-July for $1,500. His replacements Pete Conway, Bill Serad and Pete Wood, couldn't match his skill level. The Big Four kept hitting, but their opponents kept outscoring the Bisons, and the team started to lose games. As they did, the fans stayed away. Finally, on Sept. 17, 1885, Bisons President Josiah Jewett sold the franchise to a Detroit club for $7,000. The Bisons were forced to finish the schedule with local amateurs and leftovers Detroit didn't want. With the team on the way out and second-string players on the field, there was little reason for spectators to show up. During one late season game the gate receipts were only $3.00.[4]

The Buffalo Bisons re-emerged two years later, but as a minor league team in the International League. In 1890, a new major league franchise also called the Buffalo Bisons played for one season in the Player's League. The Bisons were terrible, and finished in 8th place. It would be another 24 years before Buffalo had a chance at big league baseball again. In 1914 the Buffalo Blues, formed a year earlier as a minor league team, played in the majors as part of the Federal League. The Federal League was an upstart league that tried to challenge the established American and National League's baseball dominance. When the Feds starting offering players better salaries and poaching them from the AL and NL, it was too much for these other leagues to tolerate. They bought out half of the Federal League teams including Buffalo and dismantled the league after the 1915 season.[5]

In spite of the city's failed attempts to land major league teams, the minor league Buffalo Bisons continued to play baseball. In 1889, the Bisons moved into a field at the corner of Michigan Avenue and Ferry Street, called Olympic Park, later renamed Buffalo Baseball Park. In 1924, the park was rebuilt into Bison Stadium, and in 1935 it was renamed Offermann Stadium in memory of club President Frank J. Offermann. Offermann Stadium had a capacity of 14,000, and the ballpark's atmosphere was cozy and intimate.[6] Tommy Lasorda, who was a pitcher for Montreal in the International League and later managed the L.A. Dodgers, remembered the games he played there. "Offermann Stadium was, to me, like Wrigley Field is in the majors. It was a park of togetherness."[7] Dallas Green, who pitched for the Bisons in 1959 and later became a manager with the Philadelphia Phillies and the New York Yankees, also had fond memories of the place. "Offermann was one of the great minor league ballparks of all time. The people were right on top of you, and it had the same feeling you get in Fenway. And those Buffalo fans knew their baseball."[8]

Crowd watching baseball game at Offermann Stadium, undated. Built in 1924, Offermann Stadium was the home of the minor league Buffalo Bisons until 1960, when the team moved to War Memorial Stadium (aka The Rockpile). *Photo courtesy of the Buffalo History Museum.*

Despite baseball's popularity in Buffalo, by the early 1950s the franchise was in financial trouble. On Nov. 15, 1951, team owners Marvin and Louis Jacobs sold the Bisons to the Detroit Tigers for $100,000. The deal didn't include Offermann Stadium, which was owned by Jacobs-controlled Ferry-Woodlawn Realty Corp. The contract had a reservation giving Buffalo a right of first refusal if the Tigers decided to sell the Bisons at a future date. The new owners found out some disturbing facts about the club. The team was on the verge of bankruptcy, with a debt of $326,000. This included $78,000 owed to Sportservice Corp. and $90,000 to Ferry-Woodlawn Reality Corp., both owned by the Jacobs brothers. The Detroit Tigers owners decided that, because of the team's debts, falling attendance and no suitable buyers, they would fold the franchise after the 1955 season.[9]

Taking advantage of the first refusal clause between the Detroit Tigers and Marvin and Louis Jacobs, minor league executive Joe Stigimier, Harry Bisgeier and Buffalo Evening News sports editor Bob Stedler, organized a drive to sell stock to the public to purchase the franchise. The drive succeeded, thanks to large investments by wealthy business people, including Lou Jacobs. Community ownership would pay dividends for the Bisons for the rest of the decade. The team hired talented new players including first baseman Luke Easter, the first African-American to play for the Bisons since Frank Grant in 1888, second baseman Lou Ortiz and third baseman Bill Serena. Luke Easter quickly became the Babe Ruth of Buffalo. A big man, Easter made big hits, including 114 home runs.[10]

The Buffalo Bisons played their last game at Offermann Stadium on Sept. 17, 1960. The next year, the stadium was torn down to build a junior high school. The Bisons moved to War Memorial Stadium, a concrete facility on the city's East Side that was built as a WPA project and designed for football. In fact, the new AFL Buffalo Bills would play there until 1973. War Memorial was no Offermann Stadium. Even though the place was larger, with 45,000 seats vs. 14,000, it had bad sight lines and lacked amenities like functioning restrooms.[11]

As the 1960s progressed, the sports situation in Buffalo changed. In November 1963, Sportservice Corp, which owned 67,500 of the 184,511 shares outstanding, forced out team President John Stigmier and replaced him with TV executive Van Buren DeVries.[12] It was the effective end of community ownership. New sports teams were also beginning to compete with the Bisons for fan loyalty and entertainment dollars. The upstart American Football League Buffalo Bills, which had been part of a group nicknamed the "Foolish Club" by pundits, became a proven success by the mid-1960s. College basketball games, led by rivalries between Canisius College, Niagara University and St. Bonaventure University, began to draw larger and larger crowds. In 1969, the National Hockey League awarded a new franchise to Buffalo called the Sabres. At the same time, Buffalo's economy began to weaken, with the region's heavy industrial base feeling the pinch. Combined with greater competition from other sports and a shrinking amount of money for discretionary spending, baseball in Buffalo was in trouble.

In 1968, Buffalo had an opportunity to get a major league baseball franchise, for the first time since the Buffalo Blues became part of the Federal League in 1914. Buffalo became one of the cities favored to win a National League Expansion team. This outcome looked so certain that the New York Daily News mistakenly reported that Buffalo, along with San Diego, had been awarded a new MLB team.[13] Erie County made plans to build a domed stadium in the suburbs. All these plans came to nothing, and Buffalo's baseball fans were crushed, when after some last-minute backroom lobbying, the National League awarded Buffalo's franchise to Montreal instead. Lawyer Robert Swados, who led Buffalo's effort to land a big league baseball team, expressed Buffalo fans' disappointment. "We felt, on the merits, we should have been given the franchise." He added that "Selling Buffalo was a tough job."[14]

The minor league Bisons continued to limp along, but losing a major league opportunity dampened fan interest. Opening day 1970 for the Bisons only drew 1,319 fans, the smallest in living memory. By June 2nd, the Bisons were at 9-27, and had only drawn 9,204 people to their first 13 games at home. League officials met in New York to decide what to do about the situation. On the afternoon of June 4th, the International League forfeited the Buffalo Bisons franchise and awarded it to the Montreal Expos. Montreal transferred the team to Winnipeg, Manitoba. That same day, the Bisons played their last game in Buffalo against Tidewater, and lost 7-4.[15] It was a sad end for Buffalo baseball, which had a tradition going back to the 1870s.

As the 1970s went on, it looked like baseball in Buffalo would be a thing of the past. In 1977, the voters elected Jimmy Griffin as mayor. Griffin knew that Buffalo had seen better days, but the new mayor wanted to do something to help jumpstart the city's revival. Griffin had been a lifelong baseball fan, and an amateur player. He began trying to find a way to bring a baseball team back to the once Queen City of the Great Lakes. "We were pretty far down back in those days" Griffin said later, "but I knew baseball could help this city and change the attitude of the people. All we needed was a team."[16]

In 1979, an umpire named Pete Calieri was scheduled to go to Florida for the Texas Rangers spring training camp. He had previously worked for the Double-A Eastern League, but the Triple-A International League had purchased his contract. Calieri lived in the Buffalo suburb of West Seneca. Before he left for Florida, the umpire wanted to do his taxes. So Calieri called Pat McKernan, the Eastern League's president. Calieri recalled what happened next. "I get on the phone and I start talking to Pat about my taxes. He tells me he's going to call the league accountant and then get back to me. Well, I'm getting ready to hang up, but Pat keeps talking. In the course of the conversation, he tells me the Jersey City stadium was damaged by a hurricane and is unsuitable for league play. Pat tells me he's got five teams in a six-team league."[17] Calieri offered Buffalo as a choice for a new team. When McKernan asked the umpire where the new team would play, he suggested the Rockpile, the old War Memorial Stadium. When McKernan pressed Calieri about who he could get in touch with, Calieri mentioned South Buffalo firefighter Daniel Colpoys. When McKernan contacted Colpoys, Colpoys called his friend Buffalo Mayor Jimmy Griffin.[18] With that, the wheels for a new Buffalo ball club were in motion.

After a chain of phone calls between Colpoys, Griffin, Calieri and McKernan, Pat McKernan got Mayor Griffin on the line. Griffin remembered that "I'm in my office, Pat calls and says 'Hey, how about having a team in 1980?' I said, 'Sure.' Fifteen minutes later, McKernan called again. "This time he says 'You're so enthusiastic, how about having a team this year? I said, 'Sure."[19] Even though Griffin gave his blessing for a new baseball franchise in Buffalo, he was skeptical about what he was getting into, but he decided to roll the dice and see what happened, anyway. "I didn't know what the hell I was doing. I thought to myself, 'What the hell am I doing with this baseball team?' Then I thought, 'What the hell, why not?'"[20]

Baseball was coming back to Buffalo, but it would not be easy. The team had no money, no owner, no players and no working agreement. All it had was a crumbling WPA edifice with cracking and peeling seats, grass everywhere and rust on the handrails. Most of the lights, toilets, sinks and urinals didn't work. The mayor and his partners had to fix up War Memorial Stadium in time for Opening Day, which was only two months away. Griffin decided to use community involvement and raise donations from the public, similar to the method the Bisons had used in the 1950s to stave off bankruptcy. Just as it was then, wealthy local business people would rescue Buffalo's baseball hopes. The mayor wanted to find one hundred people who would pledge one thousand dollars each. In spite of these pledges, the team still needed working capital. John Sikorski, president of the Broadway Market, lent the franchise $55,000. When the team needed a franchise fee, Sikorski wrote a check on the spot for $25,000. Sikorski's reason for supporting the new franchise was simple. "I like baseball" he said. "I just want to able to go to a game in Buffalo."[21]

With Sikorski's support, the new team got off the ground. One hurdle remained: the new ballpark had to be approved by the Pittsburgh Pirates, the parent organization of Buffalo's new Double-A baseball franchise. Branch B. Rickey, assistant director of Pittsburgh's farm clubs, grandson of the famous Brooklyn Dodgers GM, arrived to tour the site along with Pat McKernan and Stadium Director Joe Figiola. It was the middle of February, there had been a heavy snow the night before, and the temperature hovered at 20 degrees. McKernan remembered the scene. "We're walking out there in three feet of snow, stepping in holes and falling in snowdrifts. Branch is asking me what I think. I tell him, 'Don't worry, it'll be fine by April.'"[22]

Rickey wasn't so sure, but the Pirates needed a place for their new Double-A franchise to play, and he approved the site.

True to McKernan's word, the stadium was ready by April. The first season at the new site, the Buffalo Bisons drew 133,148 fans. By contrast, in 1969, the last full season the Bisons played at War Memorial, attendance was 77,708. Daniel Colpoys became general manager, and the mayor's office helped with anything he needed, including police protection. "That first year was wonderful" Colpoys recalled. "We made money, and people weren't afraid to come to the park."[23] The Bisons had a great first season, but then attendance started to slide. The 1980 team fell to a 67-70 record. The following year, it was 56-81. By 1982, attendance was down to 77,077 fans, and the franchise was $100,000 in debt. The Bisons lacked money, and no local tycoons wanted to front any more. The team was getting out-of-town offers of help, from buyers who wanted to move the franchise. Griffin and Colpoys were desperate to find a local owner who would keep the Bisons from a leaving town. A friend suggested Bob Rich, of Rich Products, Inc. a well-known and well-run frozen foods business.

On January 13, 1983, Colpoys and the Bisons' investors met with Bob Rich, Jr. at the Roosevelt Restaurant, a small establishment on the East Side that was known for serving average Joes as well as powerful politicos. The scene could not have been more outlandish. Rich and Jimmy Griffin weren't on speaking terms. The wealthy and polished mogul and the rough-and-tumble politician didn't agree on a whole lot. A partnership between the two to save baseball in Buffalo seemed highly unlikely. But the mayor realized he had few options. ""We needed somebody who could afford to run a franchise. That was the only way baseball would succeed…We were $100,000 in debt. I didn't see any other way out" Griffin recalled. Rich was surprised when Griffin reached out to him. "We got a call from the mayor's office that there were two out-of-town groups looking to buy the team and move it out of Buffalo. Mayor Griffin and I literally had a history of not agreeing with each other on anything. He's a very strong-willed guy and has his own agendas. And, I have to admit, I'm very much the same way."[25] In spite of their differences, the two men bonded over baseball and a city they both cared about and wanted to revive. Rich agreed to pitch to the investors at the Roosevelt Restaurant.

When Bob Rich arrived, and headed to a banquet room to schmooze the stockholders, a positive vote seemed far-fetched. Rich remembered that most of the investors looked befuddled, when he told them his goal was to one day bring a major league baseball team to Buffalo. One person asked him "Do you really know what you're getting into?"[26] Another demanded "Why in the world would you want to get involved with this?"[27] Rich kept his calm and projected optimism. The stockholders then decided to take a vote on whether to sell him the team, and the Rich Products owner retreated to the restaurant's bar to await the outcome. Soon after, someone came out and asked Rich to come back in. Mayor Griffin warmly shook his hand. "Congratulations, Bob, you're the new owner of the Buffalo Bisons."[28]

Buffalo Bisons owner Bob Rich, Jr., New York Gov. Mario Cuomo and Buffalo Mayor Jimmy Griffin break ground on Pilot Field, July 10, 1986. Pilot Field would replace War Memorial Stadium, where the Bisons had played on and off since 1960. *Photo by TheNewMinistry. Licensed under the Creative Commons, https://creativecommons.org/licenses/by-sa/4.0/*

The new owner and the mayor began planning for a new downtown baseball park. Their hope was it would help Buffalo land a major league franchise, something both Rich and Griffin longed for. As writer Mark Byrnes explained "The idea was, if the city could build the best baseball stadium in the country and fill it up every night, then the MLB would have no choice but to let the more sports-crazy than wealthy Buffalo have the big league team they wanted."[29] The Bisons started work on that new spectacular baseball stadium. In 1985, New York State awarded the Bisons $22.5 million to help build the new park. Mayor Griffin hired Chuck Rosenow to plan and develop it. Rosenow teamed up with Ron Labinski, an architect from Buffalo who worked in Kansas City. Labinski convinced Rosenow and the stadium committee that the new park should use Royals Stadium in Kansas City as a model. The new ballpark would be small, about 40,000 seats, and hopefully it would be filled. Rosenow said the goal was to make the Bisons "a regional franchise and reach out to small towns and to people who would bring their families to the games. The psychology was that you could have a good time at the ballpark and that you would keep coming back."[30]

Labinski soon faded from the scene, but his thinking had an impact on Rosenow and the stadium committee. Mayor Griffin, probably knowing how cold the winds off Lake Erie can be in downtown Buffalo even on warm spring days, wanted a domed stadium. Unfortunately, New York State was footing the bill and the state didn't want to pay for it. Rosenow convinced Griffin to build a 15,000-seat open air Triple-A park instead. There were other roadblocks that at times seemed insurmountable. Sportsplex, the state authority formed to decide on funding for sports projects, had a downstate majority and the lone Buffalo member, Frank Mc-Guire, spent most of his time preventing the other members from killing the project. Buffalo Common Council members wrangled over the ballpark. Councilman Al Coppola tried to defeat the bond issue for the stadium, and he even spearheaded a petition drive to place the issue on a public referendum. Thankfully for project supporters, the Erie County Board of Elections invalidated the petitions. Historic preservationists opposed the stadium until Mayor Griffin appointed a 19-member design committee to address preservation issues.[31]

The Common Council, after much political posturing and haggling, approved a stadium site at Washington and Swan streets. Construction crews broke ground in the summer of 1986, and the new Pilot Field was ready on opening day, April 14, 1988. Writer Anthony Violanti wrote that "Financially, functionally, aesthetically and symbolically, it was a grand slam."[32] The stadium came in under budget, and it featured amenities that were unheard of in most major league parks at the time, including a full-scale restaurant and a team store, specialty concessions and a massive, state-of-the-art scoreboard. Fans showed up in numbers that broke any attendance records in the history of Buffalo baseball. For the first few years after it opened, over a million fans a season poured into downtown Buffalo to watch the Bisons play.[33]

Rich, Rosenow, Griffin and their staffs had planned, designed and built a major league ballpark in the hopes that Buffalo would land a major league ball club. Pilot Field was enough to get the big league brokers' attention. In December of 1990, MLB announced its short list for expansion cities. They were Tampa-St. Petersburg, Miami, Washington, Denver, Orlando and Buffalo. Bisons owner Bob Rich said that "I'm not surprised, because Buffalo deserves this more than any other city on the list. Our dream is very much alive."[34] New York Times columnist George Vecsey agreed with Rich, that of the six cities on the list, "Buffalo is the best."[35] Baseball fans in Buffalo eagerly awaited the results of MLB's expansion franchise announcements in June of 1991, hoping Pilot Field would soon have a major league home team at last. Their hopes were dashed when Denver and Miami were given the two expansion franchises. Buffalo's hopes for a place in the majors were crushed.

One reason might have been the hefty new franchise fees. Expansion teams in 1977 had to pay only $7 million to join, but in 1991 the fee rose to $95 million,[36] more than the cost to build Pilot Field and more than the Riches, the city and the state could afford to pool together. As the 1990s went on, Major League Baseball became more and more a sport dominated by insane player salaries, luxury suite prices and big market TV deals. Bob Rich, Jimmy Griffin and host of local baseball backers gambled their hopes on landing a major league baseball team in Buffalo, and lost. What if they hadn't? What if Buffalo had become one of the MLB expansion teams in 1991? How would Buffalo's baseball scene be different today?

Milt Northrop, Buffalo News sports reporter, feels that Buffalo's best chance for landing a major league baseball franchise was in the late 1960s, when Robert Swados tried to convince the majors to award Buffalo a franchise, not the late '80s and early '90s when the Riches and Griffin made their effort. Buffalo's economy was still dominated by the steel industry, which hadn't started its decline, and the city's public image as a struggling Rust Belt locale wasn't yet established in the media. "Buffalo was still a steel town. The industrial base was not as depleted as it became later in the '70s. It didn't have a reputation as a dying Rust Belt city in the Great Lakes. That was not as firmly entrenched as it is now...Cleveland the Mistake on the Lake, the problems in Detroit and Buffalo was lumped in with all them, all the Great Lakes industrial cities who have seen better days. But old Buffalo was a great baseball town. Minor league baseball was big here and people followed it."[37]

Northrop also said that Toronto hadn't landed an MLB team yet, so Buffalo had some time to establish itself and draw fans from Canada. Toronto would have gotten the Blue Jays eventually, of course. In addition, if the multipurpose domed stadium had worked out, Buffalo could have had a home for both a major league Bisons team and an NFL Bills franchise. "The first thrust for MLB Baseball came in the (late '60s) when they went to the Dome Stadium controversy and whether it'd be a multi-purpose stadium. It was the Cottrell people, (Edward Cottrell) and they got squeezed out by San Diego and Montreal. There were some plans here to build a stadium but Montreal had no plans to build a stadium and baseball decided to go to Montreal and let them build it. They built Jarry Park stadium, I guess it was like...putting a ball field in the middle of Delaware Park on the fly."

"So, they got squeezed out there. I thought given the right circumstances base-ball would have come here and succeeded. The market's limited but also there was no team in Toronto at the time so you had Southern Ontario you could have benefitted from. I think if you were an American League franchise with the Tigers, with the Yankees, you could have developed a team here. National League I'm not so certain. This was always an American League town, it always had ties with the Detroit Tigers. There's a lot of Yankee people here."[38]

He added that, there was enough of a fan base to bring Major League Baseball here, but the Riches would have faced competition for player salaries and TV deals from big city teams, the same way franchises in San Diego, Pittsburgh and Kansas City have struggled against the larger markets. Also, a Toronto team would have sooner or later drawn off baseball fans from Southern Ontario who would other-wise come to Buffalo for big league games. "Of course, there would have been a team in Toronto eventually, so they would have to fight that battle too, for fans and for television markets. It would have been a borderline case with baseball here. I think the missed opportunity was in the '60s. The Riches were involved in trying to get a team here in the '80s, but I think they saw that it was going to be a marginal operation. I don't think they wanted to get into the same situation that Pittsburgh's been in. Kansas City is a small market team. Even San Diego fought uphill battles in dealing with the big market teams like the Yankees and the Red Sox and the Cubs. Even though the Cubs were not successful on the field, they sold out and they were an attraction and a great local TV package, too."[39]

Sal Maiorana, author and Rochester Democrat and Chronicle sports reporter, believes the economics of Major League Baseball would have made it difficult for Buffalo to support a franchise long-term. The Rich family, as wealthy as they are, don't have the resources of other owners who can pay multi-million-dollar player salaries. "The Riches were involved with that of course. They built Pilot Field with the intention of adding a second deck if a major league team ever came here. But by that point, in Buffalo's slow economy, I can't see how they could have sustained a major league baseball team. That would have been a tough one for Buffalo to handle. Salaries were already escalating out of control in baseball in the 1980s. I just don't see how Buffalo could have possibly made it work in Major League Baseball. As much as I would have loved to have seen it happen. I just don't think it would have been possible. I think Buffalo is probably a Triple-A city and it wasn't going to be anything more. They probably could have gotten a team there, the Riches could have survived for a few years I guess. But they just don't have the deep enough pockets that you need in today's game especially when you're dealing with player salaries. I just can't see Buffalo being able to do it."[40]

Maiorana also feels that the cost of moving the Buffalo Bills to downtown Buffalo would be unaffordable for the average fan, and the team should stay where it is, in Orchard Park. A downtown major league baseball operation would be out of most fans' price range, for the same reasons. "You look at the Ralph [Ed note: the Ralph is now known as Bills Stadium]. Now the ticket prices are the lowest in the NFL, parking, concessions all the lowest in the NFL. I just don't think Buffalo would have been able to afford baseball with 81 games a year. It wouldn't have been a sustainable model. I keep telling people, you want a stadium in downtown Buffalo? Here's what you're going to have to do. It's gonna cost personal seat licenses, everything, ticket prices, concessions, there won't be any tailgating. Everything will be double or triple. All these are factors that people seem to ignore. In Orchard Park, it's a great place for football. It's a great place to have games. You can keep the ticket prices manageable. And again, I just don't think that a major league baseball franchise would have worked because it doesn't make sense for the people of Buffalo to support it."[41]

Chris Ostrander, sportswriter for Two in the Box.com, agrees with Maiorana that a major league Buffalo Bisons team would have strong fan support initially, but would have struggled to be viable in the long run. The Bisons couldn't compete with other, wealthier franchises in larger cities, and the Rich family might be forced to sell the team to out-of-town owners who would move it, similar to what happened in 2004 when the Montreal Expos moved to Washington, D.C. "I think we'd be struggling in the modern-day MLB. It would have been a great civic activator. People would have loved it. I kind of liken it to almost how people feel about the Pirates, especially with their new stadium. Thankfully they had a good run there a couple years ago. When they were really bad people were still going to Pirates games with pretty good frequency, just because (they have a) beautiful stadium downtown and the whole nine yards. So, I think the support would have been pretty good."

"Not being a baseball expert but just having a general understanding of the economics, I really don't know how successful they would have been long-term especially when the really big contracts started getting signed in the early to mid 2000s. So that begs the question, how competitive they would be now or if they'd be kind of an also ran just because they'd be a budget team or if we'd be talking about relocating like Montreal did if it was just so hard to maintain them economically. Would they have wound up in D.C, would they have wound up a relocation candidate elsewhere? That's disappointing."[42]

Matt Sabuda, WBFO sports commentator, believes an MLB Bisons franchise would have great attendance its first few years, and would still have a large TV audience today. Buffalo fans love their sports, and nationally televised Bisons games would draw strong viewership in the Western New York area. However, the economics of the modern-day MLB would have ruled out a successful Buffalo team. "Buffalo is an amazing sports town. It's had a run of really bad sports years for the last 20 years and consistently we're still in the top when it comes to TV ratings across almost all sports, even sports that we don't have an interest in. Buffalo is even No. 1 in viewing for ratings for the Kentucky Derby. This is a sports town. I think that if we had a major league team here it would have been supported well. A lot of the demographics of the modern sports franchise don't find a foothold in cities like Buffalo. The name of the game is luxury suites, upselling and personal seat licenses. Buffalo, I think continues to see that as a bit of a challenge but where they struggle with that they make up for in eyeballs on TVs and just the amount of people who actually attend games."[43]

Sahlen Field in 2018. Originally opened as Pilot Field in 1988, Sahlen Field was designed to integrate with its surroundings in downtown Buffalo. Built for major league play, the ballpark featured many amenities unheard of in major league venues when it opened, including a full-scale restaurant and team store, specialty concessions and a state-of-the-art scoreboard. *Photo by Mb110888. Licensed under the Creative Commons, https://creativecommons. org/licenses/by-sa/4.0/deed.en*

Bob Rich and Jimmy Griffin's dream of a major league team calling Buffalo home may have been a pipe dream. Even so, the two civic leaders teamed up with architects, planners and baseball experts to design and build a beautiful, state-of-the-art downtown ballpark that served as a model for baseball stadiums throughout the country. Pilot Field brought fans to downtown Buffalo at a time when many people were afraid to venture away from their suburban comfort zones. Their gamble proved that if you build it, baseball fans will come, even if the MLB didn't. The economic realities of modern baseball make it difficult for a city like Buffalo to compete in the big leagues, but Bisons fans still venture to Washington and Swan streets to catch a game on warm summer days and nights, and they'll continue to do so for a long time to come.

CHAPTER 10
What if the Buffalo Braves Never Moved to San Diego?

IN THE 1960S, BUFFALO, NY, then as now, was a sports town. The only difference was the teams that fans followed were somewhat different. The Buffalo Bills were around, but they were part of the upstart American Football League, the "Foolish Club" that had yet to merge with the established National Football League. There were two teams with the name Buffalo Bisons, a minor league ball club that shared space with the Bills at War Memorial Stadium, and a minor league hockey team also called the Bisons that played at Memorial Auditorium until 1970, when a new NHL expansion team known as the Buffalo Sabres took over the hockey games. College basketball, unlike today, had a much bigger following. The college basketball rivalry of the "Little Three" Canisius College, Niagara University and St. Bonaventure University, packed in the crowds at the Aud on Saturday nights.

Former Buffalo Mayor Tony Masiello, remembered how popular Little Three college basketball games were in Buffalo. "Canisius basketball reigned supreme" he told Buffalo News sportswriter Bucky Gleason. "People don't remember the intensity and significance of Canisius and Little Three basketball on a Saturday night in the Aud. Until the Sabres and Braves came, Saturday night was owned by Canisius College. It was the night out on a Saturday night in Buffalo. Every Saturday, it was a packed house."[1]

In 1970, the National Basketball Association welcomed three new expansion teams to the league, the Portland Trailblazers, the Cleveland Cavaliers and the Buffalo Braves.[2] The entry fee for each new franchise was $3.7 million. The new Braves team was owned by a group of local investors led by Philip Ryan and Peter

Crotty. Days after the announcement was made, it became clear the local group didn't have enough cash to operate the team.[3]

Paul Snyder, the owner of Freezer Queen, a Buffalo-based frozen food products business, sold his interests in the company for $142 million and used some of the proceeds to purchase the majority of the Braves' stock. Snyder bought in as majority owner for $4 million, and he had high hopes for the new NBA team. "I was on the high of my life" he remembered. "I already owned Darien Lake. I owned a lot of real estate. So, I was on a roll. I had been an athlete in college. I knew a lot of people in sports and was friends with (Bills owner) Ralph Wilson. I followed sports."[4] The newly flush multi-millionaire decided to take over the Buffalo Braves after he went with his son to a preseason basketball game in Niagara Falls. "I take my son to Niagara Falls to see his first NBA game and the damn game goes into overtime and the Braves end up winning. It was really exciting. I decided to see if I could buy the team on the spot. It was on emotion. My son was all excited, saying, 'Dad, we got to do this', so I bought it."[5]

The Buffalo Braves had already added most of their players and staff when Paul Snyder bought majority ownership. The team's original starting five included Herm Gilliam, Don May, Dick Garrett and Nate Bowman. Bob Kauffman, a former first-round pick from Philadelphia, would become the best player that inaugural season. The franchise had hired Dolph Schayes, a Hall of Famer for the Syracuse Nationals, as the team's new coach. Eddie Donovan, former New York Knicks general manager and before that, coach at St. Bonaventure University, was the Braves' GM.[6] Snyder kept the players, coach and GM, but he otherwise cleaned house in management. He fired anyone associated with Neuberger, Loeb & Co., the New York City-based investment firm that was involved in running the Buffalo Braves.[7] On the court, the team looked like it might be off to a good start. The Braves played their season opener against the Cleveland Cavaliers at Buffalo's Memorial Auditorium on October 14, 1970. 7,129 fans attended, in a venue built to hold 15,000. The Braves won the game, 107-92. Garrett scored the first basket and a total of 20 that night. May had 24 points in 35 minutes.[8] From an investment standpoint, Snyder's impulsive purchase appeared to be a gamble that would pay dividends.

Even though the team generated some initial excitement, the Braves struggled to win games their first few seasons. The Braves finished 1970-71 with 22 wins and 60 losses, and they had a home record of 15-26. Buffalo was 4th in the NBA's Atlantic division and missed the playoffs.[9] Paul Snyder had arranged for Dolph Schayes to set up basketball clinics, to get local residents interested in the sport. However, the team's losing record wouldn't help with fan interest. Snyder knew the Braves had to get better soon. During the NBA draft in 1971, Buffalo drafted Elmore Smith, a third-round choice from Kentucky State University. The team's second pick was Fred Hilton from Grambling, a high-scoring offensive talent. For a seventh-round choice, the Braves went with Randy Smith, a local athlete who excelled at basketball, soccer and track. Smith was a consolation to local fans who hadn't forgiven the franchise for passing on Calvin Murphy, a Niagara University basketball star. At first, Randy Smith didn't look like he would do as well in the NBA as he did at Buffalo State College. But Smith proved his skeptics wrong.[10]

Braves announcer Van Miller, who went on to become a Buffalo broadcasting legend, remembered the impression Smith made on him. "Randy Smith was the perfect physical specimen. There wasn't an ounce of fat on the guy. When he was coming out of Buffalo State, a lot of people said he wasn't going to make it in the NBA...Randy was so quick that he could guard anybody. If you had an anatomy class and wanted a guy to strip down to his shorts, Randy was it."[11] Along with their new drafts, the Braves traded Don May and Herm Gilliam to Atlanta for Walt Hazzard and Jerry Chambers. In spite of their personnel moves, the Seattle Sonics annihilated the Buffalo Braves in their first season game at the Aud, 123-90. Owner Paul Snyder, his face beet red with anger and humiliation, announced at a hastily organized press conference that he was firing coach Dolph Schayes and replacing him with John McCarthy. The new coach vowed to "do everything to justify the confidence Paul Snyder and Eddie Donovan have shown in me."[12] Snyder warned his players after the press conference that "I've never been a loser and I don't intend to start with you."[13]

Randy Smith shows off his athletic skills at a photo shoot at Erie County Community College. Smith set a high school jump record of 6-feet-6-inches and had skills in college basketball, soccer, track and field. Most NBA scouts felt he lacked a dependable jump shot and the Buffalo Braves drafted him in the 7th round. Smith defied the odds and the critics and became the Braves' all-time leading scorer. *Photo courtesy of Buffalo Courier Express, Buffalo State College, Archives and Collections.*

The new coaching change didn't improve the team's winning record. The Braves finished their second season 22-60, the same as the previous year. Their home record fell slightly from 15-26 to 14-27.[14] Snyder tried different things to increase fan attendance anyway. He designed the Braves' pumpkin orange, black and white uniforms. He arranged to have the team play basketball games in Toronto, Rochester and Syracuse, to expand the fan base in Southern Ontario and Western and

Central New York. The out-of-town games drew smaller crowds than the Aud. Even so, the franchise's season ticket base grew from 600 to nearly 2,000. By late January 1971, the Braves had attracted almost 210,000 fans in 24 home games.[15] Snyder was pleased with the growing fan interest, but not with Buffalo's losing record. "Much of the time the Braves play as if hopelessly lost, disorganized and without purpose or drive" Buffalo Courier Express sportswriter Jim Baker wrote. "Sure, this is not a good team but the feeling persists that it is much better than its record indicates."[16]

Paul Snyder's coaching change didn't lead to any better results in the win column, so the owner fired coach John McCarthy after one season and replaced him with Dr. Jack Ramsay. Ramsay was a student of the game of basketball, and had a doctorate from the University of Pennsylvania. Known as a quiet leader, Ramsay accepted the Braves' coaching job with a condition. Snyder previously stormed into the team locker room and dressed down the players after a losing game. Ramsay told the owner he wouldn't take the job if Snyder kept interfering. "While I'm the coach, I need to run the team. I can't have you coming in the locker room. Snyder said, 'Oh, that's good, I think that's terrific.' For my first three years in Buffalo, he abided by that."[17] Ramsay told Snyder and GM Eddie Donovan that the Braves couldn't win with their current roster. The owner and GM went to work to change that, and Snyder set his sights on University of North Carolina star Bob McAdoo.

McAdoo had apparently signed a contract with the Virginia Squires, so he was the No. 1 pick in the American Basketball Association draft. The ABA was a serious competitor with the NBA. Because of this, the Portland Trailblazers, who had the No. 1 NBA pick, declined to pursue McAdoo. Snyder wasn't so easily rebuffed. The Braves and McAdoo's agents held secret negotiations at Buffalo's Charter House Motor Hotel. A hotel desk clerk tipped off the press, but Donovan denied that the Braves were after McAdoo, even after Buffalo Courier Express reporter Jim Baker saw Paul Snyder eating dinner with McAdoo in one of the rooms.[18]

McAdoo signed a three-year, $1 million contract with the Braves, even though, as it turned out he'd previously signed one with the Virginia Squires. After filing suit in U.S. District Court to void the Squires' contract, Snyder bought it out from the Squires for $200,000. McAdoo recalled that he signed with the NBA's Braves because that was the league where he wanted to play, and because the Braves were willing to pay him more than Portland. "The Virginia Squires and the ABA never were front and center. At first, I thought I was going to Portland as the first pick. But they didn't want to pay the money they had paid out for Sidney Wicks and Geoff Petrie, their first-round picks the previous years…I decided to sit tight and see what Buffalo did with the second pick. In the end, it all worked out."[19]

It would take a little while longer for it to work out for the Braves. In spite of the new coaching and player changes, the team finished 1972-73 21-61, only slightly better than their two previous seasons. Braves fans and supporters would have to be patient, something their impulsive owner had trouble doing. In their 4th season, the Braves finally become a serious offensive team and racked up wins. GM Donovan outbid John Y. Brown of the Kentucky Colonels to draft Ernie D. Gregorio, a passer from Providence, to the roster. The pick was a winner at the Braves' season opener, when DiGregorio passed the ball to Bob McAdoo, who made a 17-foot jump shot to beat the Houston Rockets 107-105 in overtime. It was the type of action Braves fans would get used to. McAdoo was scoring points, but Donovan added to the roster by trading John Hummer and a draft pick to the Chicago Bulls for power forward Garfield Heard and center Kevin Kunnert. The trades caused a sensation. Chicago media pundits thought the Braves got the better end of the deal. Rudy Martzke, the Braves' public relations director, took a call from Chicago Tribune writer Bob Logan. "He (Logan) said, 'Let me get this straight. Hummer for Heard, Kunnert, too. How can this be? What else is in this? Is money coming to the Bulls? Because this doesn't make any sense.'"[20]

The deals may not have made sense to the Chicago press, but they were a welcome development for Braves fans who had endured three losing seasons. Buffalo finished 1973-74 with 42 wins and 40 losses, a 24-17 home record, and made the

NBA playoffs for the first time.[21] There was another change that came in during the Braves' 4th season. Team owner Paul Snyder had announced at the end of the previous season that the Braves would play nine home games in Toronto during the following year. Snyder had previously scheduled Braves games in Rochester, Syracuse and Toronto to generate interest and attract a larger, regional fan base. His efforts had fallen flat, but he had decided to try again. Snyder reassured anxious fans and reporters, that, while he envisioned more Braves games in Toronto, the team was never leaving town. "The Braves will stay in Buffalo forever" Snyder promised, "at least as long as I own them, and I have never entertained any ideas of selling them."[22]

Bob McAdoo, center, goes for two points in the Buffalo Braves' first playoff series against the Boston Celtics, as Jo Jo White, left and Dave Cowens, right, get there a little too late. The Braves bought out McAdoo's contract from the Virginia Squires of the rival ABA. McAdoo would score more points than any other NBA player during his career. *Photo courtesy of Buffalo Courier Express, Buffalo State College, Archives and Collections.*

Milt Northrop, Buffalo News sports reporter, remembers Snyder's efforts to schedule Toronto dates as a mistake. The Braves were winning and generating fan interest in Buffalo. Moving games to Toronto made supporters in Buffalo feel Snyder had no faith in them, and the decision hurt the Braves' local following. "They (the Braves) had a couple of nice big wins. They beat the Knicks here. First time the Knicks came in, they beat 'em and that was a championship Knicks team. They beat the Lakers here on a shot at the buzzer and…it was around Christmas time. Everybody was excited. And the big story the next day was the owner talking about splitting the games with Toronto the next season. He's already talking about Toronto. What a buzzkill. Their most exciting game of the season against Wilt Chamberlin, Jerry West and Elgin Baylor and the L.A. Lakers and everybody's talking about games in Toronto? It didn't make any sense. He (Paul Snyder) did stunts like that which dampened enthusiasm. And on top of that they were competing with the sports dollar with the Sabres who came into the NHL the same year the Braves came into the NBA."[23]

The Buffalo Braves were at the top of their game in the 1974-75 season. The Braves had a winning record of 49-33, a home record of 30-11 and they finished 2nd in the Atlantic Division.[24] It was playoff time again, and Buffalo hoped to win this time, something that hadn't happened when the Braves lost to the Boston Celtics in the previous year's playoffs. Buffalo played the Washington Bullets in the first round best-of-seven series. The Braves came out hard in Game 1, beating the Bullets 113-102. The Bullets had their revenge in Game 2, when they won 120-106. The Bullets then took a 2-1 series lead in Game 3. The Braves won Game 4 and the Bullets took Game 5. Buffalo won Game 6 at home with a 102-96 victory. It was the best played game of the series. Bob McAdoo led the team in scoring with 37 points, and Jim McMillian and Randy Smith helped out with 20 and 16 points respectively. During the series, the NBA named McAdoo the league's most valuable player. However, it wouldn't be enough to defeat the Washington Bullets, who dashed the Braves' playoff hopes with a 115-96 win in Game 7.[25]

Buffalo would try again their 6th season. The Braves ended 1975-76 46-36, finished 2nd in the Atlantic Division again and had to face the Philadelphia 76ers in a best-of-three series. The Braves won the series 2-1, and faced their old nemesis, the Boston Celtics in the best-of-seven second round. Boston won the first two games at home, but Buffalo tied the series by winning the next two at home. The Celtics took Game 5 99-88 and control of the series. Buffalo suffered a disastrous loss in Game 6, where the Celtics won the best-of-seven with a 104-100 victory.[27] 25 hours after the game was over, Paul Snyder fired coach Dr. Jack Ramsay. Braves Public Relations Director Mike Shaw denied that Snyder outright fired him. "He wasn't fired, he just wasn't re-hired."[28] Randy Smith thought canning Ramsay was a mistake. "I know he had a lot of things he would like to have accomplished here. His philosophy of the game is tops. I just hope that wherever he goes he succeeds in reaching his goals. He knows the game."[29] One year later, Dr. Jack Ramsay won an NBA title as the Portland Trailblazers' coach.[30]

Big changes would be in store for the Buffalo Braves franchise, and in hindsight, not for the better. During 1976, the National Basketball Association and the American Basketball Association announced plans to merge. The NBA and ABA had been longtime competitors, but all that competition was too costly for the power brokers in both leagues. Much of the impetus for the move came from Paul Snyder and John Y. Brown, the Kentucky Colonels' owner. Snyder said that "John was in the ABA and I was in the NBA, and we got together when the leagues were trying to merge and we were having all kinds of problems. Our ability to work together, I believe, is one of the reasons that led to the merger."[31]

The NBA-ABA merger was troubling for the Braves' long-term future in Buffalo. In June 1976, around the same time as the merger, Snyder threatened to move the Braves to Hollywood, Florida unless fans bought a minimum of 5,000 season tickets for the upcoming 1976-77 season. Snyder said he had lost $3 million operating the team, and it was time for the people of Buffalo to pay up. Sabres owner Seymour Knox III said there was room enough in Buffalo for hockey, football and basketball, and implied that the Braves would do better under a different owner. John Y. Brown offered to move the Colonels to Buffalo if the Braves left, calling it one of the best basketball markets in the country. In the end, Snyder wasn't able to make good on his threat. The city of Buffalo filed a restraining order against the move, and the NBA delayed action on approving any Braves relocation. Snyder, who promised fans a few years earlier that he would never sell or move the team, pouted when he couldn't get his way.[32] "I think it is a pretty bad thing when somebody owns something and doesn't have the right to sell it. This is America and these things shouldn't happen."[33]

Snyder and the city worked out an agreement, with the Braves signing a 15-year lease at the Aud and the city agreeing to drop a $10 million lawsuit against the Braves. A key provision in the agreement allowed either the city or the team to void the lease if preseason ticket sales fell below 5,000 or ticket revenues were less than $1.625 million. Even though one Buffalo Common Council member called the deal "asinine"[34] the city went ahead with it. Soon after, Paul Snyder sold half his interest in the Braves to John Y. Brown, who became the new co-owner.[35]

Brown traded captain Jim McMillian to the New York Knicks for $500,000, and was behind the move to draft Adrian Dantley, the first-round choice from Notre Dame, and William "Bird" Averitt from the ABA dispersal draft. In late October, Brown and Snyder obtained player Moses Malone's rights from the Portland Trailblazers for $350,000. In the season opener, Malone only played for two minutes and didn't score any points or get any rebounds. Two days later the Braves traded Malone to the Houston Rockets for $100,000 and two first-round draft picks. Malone went on to play for 19 years in the NBA and was the league's MVP three times and a 12 time All Star. He also held the NBA record for the most consecutive games without fouling out.[36] Bob McAdoo disagreed with Snyder and Brown's decision to trade Malone. "Think about the front line we could have had-Moses, Dantley and myself...That would have been a front court you could have built upon for years to come. That's the kind of front-line that brings home championships."[37]

However, the new Snyder-Brown duo seemed more interested in trading talented players for draft picks, and more importantly, cash. Randy Smith recalled that "Beginning in that season, the Braves became one big revolving door with Brown having a major say in everything going on. And so many deals had a money component. It was all about the money."[38] The co-owners' willingness to trade the cream of their roster for some quick bucks meant nobody on the team was safe. That was never more apparent midway through the season when the Braves traded Bob McAdoo to the New York Knicks. McAdoo found out about it when he was Christmas shopping with Randy Smith in Toronto. Smith remembered McAdoo's shock, and how shortsighted the decision was. "Both of us couldn't believe it… We barely said a word. Snyder and Brown had decided to deal him to the Knicks of all teams…That's what really started the demise of a great, great team that we could have had up there. That great team that should have stayed together for a long, long time."[39]

Two years earlier, Snyder had tried to sue the Knicks after GM Eddie Donovan took a job as the Knicks' GM. Now suddenly, the two teams were on friendly terms. It helped that the Knicks paid Snyder and Brown $3 million for McAdoo and forward Tom McMillen in exchange for center John Gianelli. Braves fans and the Buffalo press criticized the deal, but Snyder and Brown didn't care. It was the beginning of the end of the Braves franchise.[40] Trading away some of the team's best players was bound to have an impact on the Braves' wins and losses, and it did. Buffalo finished the 1976-77 season 30-52, and dropped to 4th place in the Atlantic Division. Making the playoffs was out of the question.[41] On March 25, 1977, Paul Snyder announced that he was selling the rest of his shares in the Braves to John Y. Brown. Brown paid Snyder $4 million. Brown promised to cut ticket prices and spend more time in Buffalo, but he'd still live in Louisville. Soon after, the Knicks returned to Buffalo with former star Bob McAdoo. McAdoo scored 41 points, and the Braves failed to force an overtime.[42] A once great franchise was on its way out.

The Braves limped through the 1977-78 season and finished 27-55, with a 20-18 home record.[43] All of Brown's flurry of trades and wheeling and dealing failed to turn the team around or bring crowds back to the Aud. On May 8, 1978, John Y. Brown told the city of Buffalo the Braves' lease was broken because the franchise hadn't come close to selling 4,500 season tickets (Snyder had lowered the amount from 5,000). Many media experts thought Brown would move the team to his hometown of Louisville, but cities including Miami, San Diego, Birmingham, Minneapolis and Dallas emerged as possible candidates. On May 31st, Braves President Norm Sonju announced that the Braves were moving to Dallas and would become the Dallas Express. But just like Paul Snyder's premature move to Hollywood, Florida, negotiations hit a roadblock. Brown decided on a twenty-day postponement. By the end of June, more startling news came out. Brown had agreed to swap franchises with Boston Celtics owner Irving Levin. Levin would move the Buffalo Braves to San Diego, and Brown would own the Boston Celtics. As part of the deal, players Archibald, Knight and Barnes went to the Celtics, while the Braves received Freeman Williams, Sidney Wicks, Kevin Kunnert and Kermit Washington. In addition, Brown's Celtics kept the draft rights for college player Larry Bird. Norm Sonju became president of the Braves team in San Diego, renamed the Clippers. The city of Buffalo chose not to sue John Y. Brown or the NBA, and the NBA approved the franchise swap on July 7, 1978.[44] With that, Buffalo's eight year run with an NBA franchise was over.

What if it hadn't been? What if Paul Snyder never went to a Braves preseason game with his son and impulsively decided to buy the Braves on the spot, and John Y. Brown, who never met a trade he didn't like, never became involved? If a different owner or ownership group with foresight and a focus on winning games instead of making deals had run the Braves, how would the future of the Braves and NBA basketball in Buffalo have turned out differently?

Matt Sabuda, WBFO sports commentator, believes that if someone else instead of Paul Snyder had bought the team, the Braves would have stayed in Buffalo. The franchise needed an owner who was willing to make it work, and Snyder was the wrong person at the top. Also, it's unfortunate that Buffalo's civic leaders chose to focus on landing a major league baseball team instead of an NBA team. Basketball would have been the more successful sport in Western New York, given the chance. "I think the NBA would have been better than Major League Baseball here…It was before my time but everything I hear is that Buffalo was just a fantastic basketball town. Unfortunately, due to a series of bad financial arrangements on the part of Paul Snyder…the Braves were not really able to be competitive at the Aud…It would have been nice to see an owner who had the ability to make that franchise work and obviously, Snyder was not that guy and I think that someone (else) would have stuck with it. I think it would have been a team that would've been successful here."[45]

Chris Ostrander, sportswriter for Two in the Box.com, agrees with Sabuda that Buffalo could support an NBA franchise. Buffalo fans love their sports and a modern-day Buffalo Braves team would have a strong following in Western New York. He also feels that pro basketball is much more viable in Buffalo than an MLB team. "There was a time I (believed) Buffalo's a hockey and football town…there are no NBA fans in Buffalo. I was operating in my own personal echo chamber with no concept of what the basketball community in Buffalo and Western New York would really be like…I have amended that point of view in recent years. I think I drastically underestimated how popular basketball would be in Buffalo and I think an NBA team would do well… I think it'd be well supported. Buffalo fans just like sports, major league sports especially. The Sabres have had a tough run during bankruptcy when they were really bad. And now recently their ticket sales have finally started to decline after how many years of being terrible. But Buffalo fans… support their teams regardless of whether they're really winners. At the end of the day we're like a complete reverse bandwagon city in a sense…we just want to go to a game. So, I think an NBA team would have done very well…An MLB team would do very well. I just don't think the MLB team would compete. But I think

…all the things that Buffalo could use a second go around on, I've got to think it's basketball more so than baseball, just in my view."[46]

Milt Northrop feels that, long-term, the Braves would have had a tough time competing with the Sabres, asking fans to pay ever increasing ticket costs, which would have priced basketball games out of reach for the average fan. "It would have been tough with hockey still here…for both to succeed. One reason is because of ticket pricing, it's just so high…people go to the Sabres games, I don't know how they do it. I see people sitting there, a father, mother, sitting there with kids… there's four seats there, that's like $400 worth of tickets. How do people afford this? How they afford it 40 odd games a year I don't know. Now you add basketball on top of that; I don't know how you do it."[47]

Northrop recalls a basketball game he went to in Boston in the early '90s, and prices were already high. He remembers musing that fans in Buffalo would have stayed home rather than pay similar costs if they still had an NBA team. "In the '90s I was in Boston…for something else…when the Pistons were playing the Celtics at the old Boston Garden. Somebody offered me tickets. So, I said yeah, I'd love to go to the game. So, we went to the game, got there late because it was a slow start…and the tickets were complimentary but they were $45. This is 1993…And they were not great seats, it was…looking on the end line into the court."

"I said, "Wow", I don't think people in Buffalo would pay $45 to see a basketball game and that was back then. Now those seats would probably be $90. So, I think the game would price itself out in Buffalo especially if it was competing with the National Hockey League which was pretty entrenched when they came here."[48]

Northrop is also of the opinion that the NBA wasn't fair to the Braves during their first draft year in 1970. As a new expansion team, the Braves should have had their pick of better players to generate fan interest. They also made the mistake of passing on Calvin Murphy, a missed opportunity. "The NBA was not very fair in the…college draft that year (1970) which was probably…the deepest best draft in the history of the NBA…when Buffalo came in and they made some decisions drafting that hurt. That was a great draft. The NBA was involved and some of the top players went into the NBA in those years. But that was the year Pete Maravich, Bob Lanier, Dave Cowens, Rudy Tomjanovich, Nate Archibald, Calvin Murphy, Garfield Heard, Jim McMillan, it was a super draft that year. And we end up with John Hummer. They probably should have taken Calvin Murphy; at least he would have had the game in charge. A great player."

Paul Snyder told Buffalo News sportswriter Bucky Gleason that the main reason the Braves left Buffalo was because he couldn't get weekend dates at the Aud for the Braves. The Buffalo Sabres had their choice of dates, and Canisius College got their choice of the remaining dates for college basketball games. The Braves had to wait to make their schedule until the Sabres and Canisius finished theirs. Snyder said he offered Canisius President Father James Demske $125,000 if he would give up certain Saturday night dates to the Braves, but Demske declined. According to Snyder, this was the primary factor in the Braves moving to San Diego. Snyder also believed Buffalo couldn't support both the Sabres and the Braves, and if the Braves hadn't moved, the Sabres would have. Former NBA Commissioner David Stern agreed with Snyder. "The economics of the team at that time and in that market did not work. If you have a basketball and hockey team in the same building under the same ownership, that's one thing. But when they're competing with each other for dates, whichever team is in second place is severely disadvantaged."[49]

Milt Northrop blames the NBA, and David Stern especially, for not giving Buffalo a chance. Buffalo suffered for being in a northern location, because Stern was fixated on basketball's future in the South and West, and he ignored Snyder and Brown's mismanagement. "Buffalo had no friends in the NBA as far as the commissioner's office...Larry O'Brien was the commissioner but David Stern was his right-hand guy at the time. David Stern was not a northern cities guy, he was a Sun Belt guy. He had designs on the Sun Belt and the West...They had no friends here to stand up to what Snyder and John Y. Brown pulled here."[50]

Sal Maiorana, author and Rochester Democrat and Chronicle sports reporter, disagrees with Snyder and Stern that dates were the issue. At the time in the 1970s, the Sabres never played home games on Saturday nights. Canisius didn't play every game at home, and there were enough road game dates for Canisius the Braves could have taken. Also, the college basketball season ended earlier than the NBA, which gave the Braves extra days at the end of the season they could have picked up. "I always thought that was complete bullsh*t (that Canisius didn't want to share game times with the Braves). Canisius was in the Aud on Saturday nights. I went back and took a look at the research. They were in there maybe eight, nine, ten Saturdays a year. So, the NBA season goes from early October to whatever for the playoffs, right? There were plenty of Saturdays that the Aud would have been available because the Sabres never played on Saturday nights. Back then it was usually Thursday and Sunday that they were playing at the Aud. So, the whole Canisius thing was a crock of sh*t. You could have played on Friday nights when Canisius had it for Saturday. And then once their college basketball season was over which was usually the start of March, there was plenty of time to have the Braves play Saturday night games."[51]

Northrop said that college basketball in Buffalo was in trouble in the 1960s and '70s. Teams stopped coming to Buffalo to play doubleheaders, as every college and university started building large arenas and no longer needed venues like Buffalo's Memorial Auditorium. Also, a financial fight between Canisius College and Niagara University that lasted most of the 1960s dampened fan interest in the "Little Three" because only St. Bonaventure played with any consistency at the Aud during that decade. "Teams used to come into Buffalo on their way to New York City, stop here and play a doubleheader. They won't do that anymore because... everybody built big field houses and big arenas on campus. They weren't going to give up a road date to share a game four ways in Buffalo when they could travel to some other school that has a 15,000-seat arena and get 40% of the gate or whatever they negotiate."

"By then in the '60s, Canisius and Niagara had a fight. Many people forget about that. Canisius and Niagara did not play each other for eight years. And that was a guaranteed 12,000 fans at the Aud that they split twice a year…every year. I don't think the Gallagher Center was open at Niagara until early '60s but they just kissed that goodbye because they were fighting over money and the only thing that kept the doubleheader programs alive in the '60s in the Aud was St. Bonaventure. Before they built the Reilly Center they would play (at the Aud) and UB played some mid-major games on a doubleheader with Canisius. But Niagara dropped out of the doubleheader program altogether. College basketball was heading for a downhill slide…in Buffalo."[52]

Maiorana doesn't believe that Aud managers and team owners couldn't have worked out an arrangement between the Sabres, Canisius College and the Braves. Many other arenas in other cities manage to do it, including New York City's Madison Square Garden and Los Angeles' Staples Center. "Madison Square Garden is able to host events basically every night…Between the Knicks, the Rangers and all the other stuff that's held at Madison Square Garden. They manage just fine. So, there's no reason why the Sabres, the Braves and Canisius College couldn't find a way to make that work. I really will never understand the logic there. Madison Square Garden is the busiest arena I can think of. Maybe the Staples Center in L.A. is probably busier because they've got the Kings, the Clippers, the Lakers plus everything else…Staples Center and Madison Square Garden are probably the two busiest arenas in America and they make it work. You're telling me Buffalo couldn't make it work with the Sabres, the Braves and Canisius? Which were only playing for eight or ten games anyway? I don't get it."[53]

Milt Northrop thinks the Braves didn't do enough to market the team in Buffalo, and the Braves could have been successful with Friday night and Sunday afternoon games, which were available and worked when the Braves did play those times. "I don't think the Braves did the best they could to market the team here. For instance, they hardly ever played…Sunday afternoon family type games but they did that a couple times and they did well. They played Friday and they only played a few Saturday night games before the Canisius College season started. Then they were left with Friday nights. And I think they could have succeeded with Friday nights and Sunday afternoons but they didn't do that. Paul Snyder complained about not being able to get into the Aud on Saturday nights and he thought that all the high school basketball on Friday nights was hurting his chances of getting a big gate."[54]

Northrop also believes, along with Maiorana that Aud dates weren't an issue. Snyder used that as an excuse, even though as Northrop and Maiorana already pointed out, Snyder had Sundays and Fridays available, had he chosen to schedule more games during those time slots. "That's his crutch (that Snyder couldn't make it because he couldn't get the good nights at the Aud). Bucky Gleason did a story about it a couple of years ago and he fell for Snyder's crying hook, line and sinker. He (Snyder) didn't utilize the dates that were available to the best of them. All he did was complain about the thing and as it turned out, they wouldn't have driven Canisius out (of the Aud) which they ended up doing. They would have driven Canisius right out of the basketball business and sent them to the Koessler Center which ended up happening anyway."[55]

Tim Wendel, author of Buffalo: Home of the Braves, feels that the Braves' owners weren't patient enough to wait a little longer and build a long-term franchise. John Y. Brown, especially, wasn't willing to build a team and traded away the Braves' best players. The fans were supportive, and players loved their time in Western New York. It's just unfortunate that the Paul Snyder and John Y. Brown weren't as committed to a basketball franchise in Buffalo as the players and fans had been. "They needed a little bit more to get them over the top. I think a top line with (Moses) Malone, (Bob) McAdoo and (Adrian) Dantley would have done it. Unfortunately, they had ownership that was (dysfunctional), certainly that weird 50-50 percent between Paul Snyder and John Y. Brown. John Y. Brown liked ABA type of players, the teams coming from Kentucky and the Kentucky Colonels and they just seemed unable to have the patience to just let things be for a bit and see what they had. And I think it would've been...apparent pretty quickly that that front line that I just spoke of would have been pretty good. A little bit more patience, a little bit more foresight, the Braves would still be in Buffalo, and I'm pretty sure would have won a championship by now."[56]

Northrop agrees with Wendel that Paul Snyder was a short-term investor who wasn't farsighted enough to build a long-term team in Western New York. Even after the Braves moved to San Diego, they moved again to L.A. and it took 15 years before the new franchise known as the L.A. Clippers was financially viable in Los Angeles. Snyder didn't want to wait, and the outsiders he brought in killed Buffalo's NBA future. "Eventually Snyder and the NBA would have dominated the market for basketball, but Snyder was still impatient. My theory about Snyder was he was an ambitious businessman and investor and he had his money tied up in the NBA team and he wanted...to get money out of the team and move to some other ventures. That's why he brought in John Y. Brown and Harry Magurian, who was a furniture guy from Rochester...Once they brought those people in, who were not Buffalo people, had no faith in the town and designs to go, the franchise was gone. It was on its way out. And a lot of the public believed that and nobody could do anything about it."

"I also think they missed the dawning of the great NBA Era with (Larry) Bird and (Magic) Johnson coming in and the great Philadelphia 76er teams, the Lakers-Celtics rivalry they missed, because they bailed out before it happened. And San Diego was a failure. It took them to finally move the team to L.A. and even then, it took 15 years in L.A. for the team to be successful."[57]

Wendel believes that, had the Braves had stayed around for a few more years, the team would have enjoyed an ever-increasing popularity. The NBA in the Buffalo Braves Era wasn't as big as it would be in the years to come. "I think they kind of gave up a little bit too early because there were a whole lot more bigger things coming into play in the sports landscape which is going to change markedly and it certainly did in the '80s and into the '90s. Even the NBA, you look at the NBA when the Braves were playing...it certainly wasn't the NBA now. I can still remember Magic Johnson winning a championship with the Lakers not too long after this and they were showing the games on tape delay. I mean that's how the NBA really had no vibe, no buzz. So, you put all those things together again. I'm not losing money in the thing, I'm not the owner. But there were some major influences and sea changes coming relatively quickly that I think would have benefitted the Braves and Buffalo immensely."[58]

Maiorana agrees with Wendel and Northrop that a different owner who was a little more patient would have had to wait just a few years before the NBA took off. In the meantime, the Braves were drawing large crowds to their games. Mismanagement from the owners, not bad dates or lack of fan interest, is what ultimately killed the franchise. "The Braves needed two or three years because once Magic (Johnson) and (Larry)Bird came into the league the NBA took a quantum leap forward and the Braves I think would have been able to make it a go… If Snyder had sold the team to an ownership group…that would have stayed patient and kept the team in Buffalo, there's no reason why they couldn't have survived for years and years alongside the Sabres, first at the Aud and later at KeyBank Center…If they could have gotten to the crest of that wave when Magic and Bird came on the scene, I think the Braves would probably still be in Buffalo today. Or at the very least, they would have survived a long, long time. It was just a shame that the planets just didn't quite align for the Braves because they had a great following. The Braves got good, they really packed 'em in. They had 16,000 into that building on some nights. It was great, a lot of fun. It was a fun team to watch."[59]

The players who spoke to Tim Wendel regret how the Braves' time in Buffalo ended. Shortsighted owners, city leaders and the NBA all contributed. "Every player I talked to in doing Buffalo Home of the Braves, loved playing in Buffalo and they still (do), it was and is a great sports city. And all of them felt the NBA, forces beyond ownership's control, lack of ownership foresight (did the Braves in). The ones that got screwed in the end were the fans because they felt they had great fans there. They loved playing in the old Aud."[60]

Wendel said that Buffalo's politicians, along with key people in the NBA, are as much to blame as Paul Snyder and John Y. Brown for the Braves moving to San Diego. Buffalo's politicos didn't seem to care if the city had a pro basketball team or not. "I find it interesting to this day that the guy who brokered that deal (to swap the Braves and Celtics) is David Stern and he goes on to become commissioner. And even look at the city fathers in Buffalo and you look today at how cities will really make it tough for a team to leave. I mean they'll fight them in court; they'll do whatever it takes. And then for the city to sign that kind of ridiculous (lease) I believe it was 5,000 season tickets had to be sold or else we'll wipe out the lease that the team had with the city, the Aud. I mean first of all to sign that is ridiculous. And then secondly the team is going out the door, and you don't fight it anymore. It's almost like...don't let the door hit you on the way out. And you don't realize really what you've lost as a city until they're gone. They (players) really were a bit perplexed why the city government didn't fight to keep the Braves there. It would have worked."[61]

Tim Wendel pointed out that a successful Braves franchise would draw fans to downtown Buffalo on a regular basis. Braves fans, along with Sabres spectators, could have created a critical mass that jumpstarted Buffalo's redevelopment boom decades before HarborCenter and Canalside. Sports can contribute to any city's revival, and the Braves would be part of Buffalo's civic renaissance. "Sports isn't a cure all for everything. But if you get enough vibrancy from sports and other things in the downtown corridor it invigorates it much quicker. I was just up in Buffalo maybe a couple months ago and I was really heartened by how much the downtown had come around. I found myself thinking boy, this could have been like this maybe 20, 25 years earlier if some certain things were placed there as opposed to...the Bills playing in Orchard Park if the Bills had been downtown. So, who knows. And maybe if the Braves are still around, the Braves are winning and that helps that energy, that synergy a little bit more."[63]

If Paul Snyder hadn't bought the Buffalo Braves on a whim and the team had a more patient and farsighted owner, the franchise might not have moved to San Diego. Certainly, if John Y. Brown didn't come into the picture the Braves would have far more likely stayed in Western New York. Or, if the Buffalo Common Council had insisted on a stronger lease like the one Erie County signed with the Bills that made it difficult for them to move, the Clippers could still be the Braves. Also, if certain people were willing to compromise, on season ticket sales, on foregoing short-term profits, basketball fans might still head downtown to catch a game the way they do in other cities. Buffalo is a sports town, with die-hard fans, and it's unfortunate that pro basketball isn't part of that sports landscape today.

NOTES

CHAPTER ONE NOTES

1. "History of the St. Louis Rams." Wikipedia. Aug. 29, 2018. https://en.wikipedia.org/wiki/History_of_the_St._Louis_Rams

2. Schrotenboer, Brent. "Winners and losers of all the NFL relocation." USA Today, Mar. 28, 2017. Accessed Aug. 29, 2018. https://www.usatoday.com/story/sports/nfl/2017/03/28/las-vegas-raiders-relocation-los-angeles-rams-chargers/99721134/

3. Graham, Tim. "Why the Bills Won't Go Hollywood." The Buffalo News. May 28, 2014.

4. Thomas, Jim. "Suit alleges litany of false statements by Kroenke, Demoff, Goodell." Stltoday.com. Apr. 13, 2017. Accessed April 22, 2020. https://www.stltoday.com/sports/football/professional/suit-alleges-litany-of-false-statements-by-kroenke-demoff-goodell/article_38257d09-a38b-551e-9ee1-7fde6f5804b0.html "approved excerpts © (2017), St. Louis Post Dispatch"

5. Thomas, Jim. (Apr. 13, 2017) "approved excerpts © (2017), St. Louis Post Dispatch"

6. Thomas, Jim. (Apr. 13, 2017) "approved excerpts © (2017), St. Louis Post Dispatch"

7. Thomas, Jim. "St. Louis suing NFL over Ram's relocation." Stltoday.com. Apr. 13, 2017. Accessed April 22, 2020. https://www.stltoday.com/sports/football/professional/st-louis-suing-nfl-over-rams-relocation/article_501e2349-c9c9-5a70-9743-2583f89948d9.html "approved excerpts © (2017), St. Louis Post Dispatch"

8. Graham, Tim. (May 28, 2014).

9. Fenno, Nathan and Farmer, Sam. "NFL Teams often use L.A. to get better deals to stay where they are." Los Angeles Times. Jan. 6, 2015. Accessed Aug. 29, 2018. http://www.latimes.com/sports/nfl/la-sp-la-leverage-city-20150107-

story.htm. Nathan Fenno, Sam Farmer Copyright © 2015 Los Angeles Times. Used with permission.

10. Schrotenboer, Brent. (Mar. 28, 2017). "excerpt © 2017 by Kitty Ratcliffe. Used with permission."

11. Hanzus, Dan. "Rams relocate to L.A.: Chargers first option to join." NFL. com. Jan. 12, 2016. Accessed Aug. 30, 2018. http://www.nfl.com/news/story/0ap3000000621645/article/rams-to-relocate-to-la-chargers-first-option-to-join

12. Hanzus, Dan. (Jan. 12, 2016).

13. Schrotenboer, Brent. (Mar. 28, 2017).

14. Zremski, Jerry. "Wilson's intent for Bills is mystery." The Buffalo News. Aug. 1, 2014.

15. McCarthy, Robert and Precious, Tom. 'Governor doubtful on new stadium." The Buffalo News. June 25, 2014.

16. Schrekinger, Ben. "Inside Donald Trump's Shady Scheme to Keep Jon Bon Jovi From Buying the Buffalo Bills." GQ.com. Oct. 26, 2017. Accessed Aug. 30, 2018. https://www.gq.com/story/donald-trump-shady-scheme-to-buy-nfl-buffalo-bills "Ben Schrekinger, GQ@Condé Nast."

17. Schrekinger, Ben. (Oct. 26, 2017). "Ben Schrekinger, GQ@Condé Nast."

18. Schrekinger, Ben. (Oct. 26, 2017). "Ben Schrekinger, GQ@Condé Nast."

19. Schrekinger, Ben. (Oct. 26, 2017). "Ben Schrekinger, GQ@Condé Nast."

20. Dudzik, Kelly. "Bars Ban Bon Jovi to Support Bills Staying in Buffalo." Wgrz. com. May 22, 2014. Accessed May 21, 2020. https://www.wgrz.com/article/sports/nfl/bills/bars-ban-bon-jovi-to-support-bills-staying-in-buffalo/314263382

21. Bills Fan Thunder. Originally posted on Facebook, May 2014. https://www.facebook.com/groups/662030030545332/

22. Florio, Mike. "Jaworski says Bon Jovi wouldn't move the Bills out of Buffalo." NBC Sports.com. June 30, 2014. Accessed Aug. 30, 2018. https://profootball-

talk.nbcsports.com/2014/06/30/jaworski-says-bon-jovi-wouldnt-move-the-bills-out-of-buffalo/

23. Florio, Mike. (June 30, 2014)."Courtesy of Pro Football Talk/NBC Sports."

24. Graham, Tim. "In letter, Bon Jovi vows to keep Bills in the region." The Buffalo News. Aug. 3, 2014.

25. Graham, Tim. (Aug. 3, 2014).

26. Zremski, Jerry. 'Bills fans don't buy Bon Jovi's letter." The Buffalo News. Aug. 4, 2014.

27. Zremski, Jerry. (Aug. 4, 2014).

28. Ray, Jay and Graham, Tim. "Rai denies being involved with the Toronto group's ownership bid." The Buffalo News. Aug. 15, 2014.

29. Ray, Jay and Graham, Tim. (Aug. 15, 2014).

30. News staff reports. "Bon Jovi reportedly out of group eyeing Bills, Toronto bidders think move improves chances." The Buffalo News. Aug. 30, 2014.

31. Graham, Tim. Precious, Tom and Zremski, Jerry. "Thanks a billion, Pegulas submit an aggressive $1.4 billion bid to acquire Buffalo Bills franchise. The Buffalo News. Sept. 10, 2014.

32. Fink, James. Pegula: 'We all just bought a football team...our team, the Buffalo Bills.' Bizjournals.com. Oct. 10, 2014. Accessed April 25, 2020. https://www.bizjournals.com/buffalo/news/2014/10/10/pegula-we-all-just-bought-a-football-team-our-team.html

33. Staff. "Transcript of Terry Pegula's first news conference as Bills owner." The Buffalo News. Oct. 10, 2014. Accessed April 25, 2020. https://buffalonews.com/2014/10/10/transcript-terry-pegulas-first-news-conference-bills-owner/

34. Miller, Jeffrey (author, Buffalo Bills historian) in discussion with the author. July 19, 2018.

35. Graham, Tim. (former Buffalo News sports reporter, senior writer at The Athletic) in discussion with the author. Feb. 25, 2019.

36. Graham, Tim. (Feb. 25, 2019).

37. Mairoana, Sal. (author, Rochester Democrat and Chronicle sports reporter) in discussion with the author. July 9, 2018.

38. Sabuda, Matthew (Buffalo Fan Alliance President, WBFO sports commentator) in discussion with the author. Aug. 15, 2018.

39. Ostrander, Chris (sportswriter, Two in the Box.com) in discussion with the author. Aug. 14, 2018.

40. Maiorana, Sal. (July 9, 2018).

41. Maiorana, Sal. (July 9, 2018).

42. O'Shei, Tim. "What if the Bills had been dealt a Trump card?" The Buffalo News. Nov. 5, 2016. Accessed Aug. 31, 2018. https://buffalonews. com/2016/11/05/trump-bought-buffalo-bills-oral-history-alternate-reality/

43. O'Shei, Tim. (Nov. 5, 2016).

44. O'Shei, Tim. (Nov. 5, 2016).

45. O'Shei, Tim. (Nov. 5, 2016).

46. Graham, Tim. (Feb. 25, 2019).

47. Ostrander, Chris (Aug. 14, 2018).

48. Ostrander, Chris (Aug. 14, 2018).

49. Ostrander, Chris (Aug. 14, 2018).

Chapter Two Notes

1. "Super Bowl XXV." Wikepedia. Accessed Sept. 5, 2018. https://en.wikipedia. org/wiki/Super_Bowl_XXV

2. Pitoniak, Scott. "The Bad." In The Good, the Bad, the Ugly Buffalo Bills. Chicago: Triumph Books, 2007. 48.

3. Rush, Doug, "On this date: New York Giants beat Buffalo Bills in Super Bowl XXV." USA Today.com. Jan. 27, 2018. Accessed Sept. 8, 2018. https:// giantswire.usatoday.com/2018/01/27/new-york-giants-buffalo-bills-super-bowl-xxv-on-this-date/

4. Fazzolari, Brandon. "51 Super Bowls in 51 Days-Super Bowl XXV." Boston Sports Extra.com. Jan. 8, 2018. Accessed Sept. 8, 2018. http://bostonsportsextra.com/nfl/2018/01/51-super-bowls-51-days-super-bowl-xxv

5. Kramer, McKenzie. "NFL-The against-the-spread gambling result from every Super Bowl." ESPN.com. Feb. 6, 2018. Accessed Sept. 5, 2018. http://www.espn.com/chalk/story/_/id/18592627/nfl-spread-gambling-result-every-super-bowl

6. Oates, Bob. "Super Bowl XXV/New York Giants vs. Buffalo Bills." Los Angeles Times. Jan. 26, 1991. Accessed Sept. 5, 2018. http://articles.latimes.com/1991-01-26/sports/sp-496_1_super-bowl-xxiBob Oates Copyright © 1991 Los Angeles Times. Used with permission.

7. Gola, Hank. "Super Bowl XXV Rewind: Giants beat Buffalo Bills in a game where it all went right for Big Blue." New York Daily News. Feb. 5, 2011. Accessed Sept. 5, 2018. http://www.nydailynews.com/sports/football/giants/super-bowl-xxv-rewind-giants-beat-buffalo-bills-game-big-blue-article-1.136184

8. Gola, Hank. (Feb. 5, 2011).

9. Gola, Hank. (Feb. 5, 2011).

10. Sarni, Jim and Bricker, Charles. "Pregame, Halftime Shows To Pay Tribute To America." SunSentinel. Jan. 27, 1991. Accessed Sept. 5, 2018. http://articles.sun-sentinel.com/1991-01-27/sports/9101050624_1_gasparilla-buffalo-fan-super-bowl-xxv

11. Sneed, Bradon. "Before the Hoodie: Bill Belichick's Origin Story." Bleacher Report.com. Sept. 10, 2015. Accessed Aug. 10, 2018. https://bleacherreport.com/articles/2554417-before-the-hoodie-bill-belichicks-origin-story

12. Vacchiano, Ralph. "The Genius of Little Bill: Belichick's Super Bowl XXV game plan with Giants is stuff of legend. " New York Daily News, Nov. 14, 2015. Accessed Aug. 10, 2018. http://www.nydailynews.com/sports/football/giants/bill-belichick-super-bowl-xxv-game-plan-stuff-legend-article-1.2435400#

13. "Super Bowl XXV." Wikepedia. Accessed Sept. 8, 2018. https://en.wikipedia.org/wiki/Super_Bowl_XXV

14. "Super Bowl XXV." Wikepedia.

15. "Super Bowl XXV." Wikepedia.

16. "Super Bowl XXV." Wikepedia.

17. "Super Bowl XXV." Wikepedia.

18. "Super Bowl XXV." Wikepedia.

19. Pitoniak, Scott. "The Bad." In The Good, the Bad, the Ugly Buffalo Bills. Chicago: Triumph Books, 2007. 47.

20. Pitoniak, Scott. (2007). 47.

21. Pitoniak, Scott. (2007). 47.

22. Gagnon, Brad. "Wide Right 25 Years Later: A Super Bowl So Much Larger Than Just Scott Norwood." Bleacher Report.com. Jan. 27, 2016. Accessed Sept. 8, 2018. https://bleacherreport.com/articles/2607652-wide-right-25-years-later-a-super-bowl-so-much-larger-than-just-scott-norwood

23. Miller, Jeffrey (author, Buffalo Bills historian) in discussion with the author. July 19, 2018.

24. Mairoana, Sal. (author, Rochester Democrat and Chronicle sports reporter) in discussion with the author. July 9, 2018.

25. Sabuda, Matt. (WBFO Sports Commentator) in discussion with the author. Aug. 15, 2018.

26. Ostrander, Chris. (sportswriter, Two in the Box.com) in discussion with the author. Aug. 14, 2018.

27. Ostrander, Chris. (Aug. 14, 2018).

28. Graham, Tim. (former Buffalo News sports reporter, senior writer at The Athletic) in discussion with the author. Feb. 25, 2019.

29. Sneed, Bradon. (Sept. 10, 2015).

30. Halberstram, David. "Chapter Eleven." In The Education of a Coach. New York: Hyperion, 2005. 202. From The Education of a Coach. by David Halber-

stram., copyright © 2005. Reprinted by permission of Hyperion., an imprint of Hachette Book Group, Inc.

31. Sneed, Bradon. (Sept. 10, 2015).

32. Graham, Tim. (Feb. 25, 2019).

33. Curry, George E. "City and Bills' Fans Exhibit Super Class, Despite A Giant Loss." Chicago Tribune, January 29, 1991. Accessed August 10, 2018. http://articles.chicagotribune.com/1991-01-29/news/9101090317_1_buffalo-residents-scott-norwood-super-bowl-xxv

34. Curry, George E. (Jan. 29, 1991).

35. Curry, George E. (Jan. 29, 1991).

36. BWW News Desk. "New Play Imagines The Buffalo Bills As Super Bowl Champs." Broadway World.com. May 2, 2018. Accessed Sept. 10, 2018. https://www.broadwayworld.com/buffalo/article/New-Play-Imagines-The-Buffalo-Bills-As-Super-Bowl-Champs-20180502

Chapter Three Notes

1. "O.J. Simpson." Wikedpedia.com. Accessed Sept. 10. 2018. https://en.wikipedia.org/wiki/O._J._Simpson

2. "1983 NFL Draft." Wikepedia.com. Accessed Sept. 10, 2018. https://en.wikipedia.org/wiki/1983_NFL_Draft

3. Maun, Tyler. "Before the Broncos, Elway Eyed the Bronx." MiLB.com. Mar. 12, 2015. Accessed Sept. 10, 2018. https://www.milb.com/milb/news/before-the-broncos-elway-eyed-the-bronx/c-112011776

4. Brown, Chris. "Bills All-Time draft memories: Jim Kelly." Buffalo Bills.com. Apr. 6, 2010. Accessed Aug. 6, 2020. https://www.buffalobills.com/news/bills-all-time-draft-memories-jim-kelly-2211851

5. Brown, Chris. (Apr. 6, 2010).

6. Brown, Chris. (Apr. 6, 2010).

7. Web Staff. "How Jim Kelly became a Houston Gambler." CW39.com. July 24,

2017. Accessed Sept. 11, 2018. https://cw39.com/2017/07/24/how-jim-kelly-became-a-houston-gambler/

8. Cichon, Steve. "The story of how Jim Kelly hated Buffalo before he loved it." Buffalo Stories.com. Dec. 17, 2017. Accessed Sept. 10, 2018. http://blog.buffalostories.com/the-story-of-how-jim-kelly-hated-buffalo-before-he-loved-it/

9. Cichon, Steve. (Dec. 17, 2017).

10. "Jim Kelly." Wikepedia.com. Accessed Sept. 11, 2018. https://en.wikipedia.org/wiki/Jim_Kelly

11. Argovitz, Dr. Jerry and Miller, J. David. "Small Potatoes, My Ass..." In Super Agent: The One Book the NFL & NCAA Don't Want You to Read. New York: Sports Publishing, 2013. 303.

12. Markazi, Arash. "Five things to know about Donald Trump's USFL experience." ESPN.com. July 14, 2015. Accessed Sept. 11, 2018. http://www.espn.com/espn/story/_/id/13255737/five-things-know-donald-trump-usfl-experience

13. Markazi, Arash. (July 14, 2015).

14. Telander, Rick. "Life with Lord Jim. Is New Jersey's Jim Kelly Pro football's Best Quarterback? He could be, and there's little doubt he is having the most fun." Sports Illustrated. July 21, 1986. Accessed Sept. 11, 2018. https://www.si.com/vault/1986/07/21/113680/life-with-lord-jim-is-new-jerseys-jim-kelly-pro footballs-best-quarterback-he-could-be-and-theres-little-doubt-that-he-is-having-the-most-fun "Reprinted courtesy of SPORTS ILLUSTRATED: "Life with Lord Jim: Is New Jersey's Jim Kelly Pro Football's Best Quarterback? He Could Be, and There's Little Doubt That He Is Having the Most Fun", by Rick Telander, July 21, 1986. Copyright © 2020. ABG-SI LLC. All rights reserved."

15. Markazi, Arash. (July 14, 2018).

16. Telander, Rick. (July 21, 1986). "Reprinted courtesy of SPORTS ILLUSTRATED: "Life with Lord Jim: Is New Jersey's Jim Kelly Pro Football's Best Quar-

terback? He Could Be, and There's Little Doubt That He Is Having the Most Fun", by Rick Telander, July 21, 1986. Copyright © 2020. ABG-SI LLC. All rights reserved."

17. Telander, Rick. (July 21, 1986). "Reprinted courtesy of SPORTS ILLUSTRAT-ED: "Life with Lord Jim: Is New Jersey's Jim Kelly Pro Football's Best Quar-terback? He Could Be, and There's Little Doubt That He Is Having the Most Fun", by Rick Telander, July 21, 1986. Copyright © 2020. ABG-SI LLC. All rights reserved."

18. Markazi, Arash. (July 14, 2015).

19. Fink, James. "Buffalo Eagles? Philadelphia Bills? It might have happened, book says." Buffalo Business First. Dec. 17, 2017. Accessed Sept. 11, 2018. https://www.bizjournals.com/buffalo/news/2017/12/11/buffalo-eagles-phila-delphia-bills-it-might-have.html

20. Pitoniak, Scott. "The Good." In The Good, the Bad, the Ugly Buffalo Bills. Chicago: Triumph Books, 2007. 23.

21. Pitoniak, Scott. (2007). 23.

22. Pitoniak, Scott. (2007). 23.

23. Pitoniak, Scott. (2007). 23.

24. Pitoniak, Scott. (2007). 23.

25. Pitoniak, Scott. "The Good." In The Good, the Bad, the Ugly Buffalo Bills. Chicago: Triumph Books, 2007. 25.

26. Pitoniak, Scott. (2007). 25.

27. Pitoniak, Scott. "The Good." In The Good, the Bad, the Ugly Buffalo Bills. Chicago: Triumph Books, 2007. 22.

28. Pitoniak, Scott. (2007). 22.

29. Pitoniak, Scott. "The Good." In The Good, the Bad, the Ugly Buffalo Bills. Chicago: Triumph Books, 2007. 25-26.

30. Miller, Jeffrey (author, Buffalo Bills historian) in discussion with the author. July 19, 2018.

31. Maiorana, Sal. (author, Rochester Democrat and Chronicle sports reporter) in discussion with the author. July 9, 2018.

32. Maiorana, Sal. (July 9, 2018).

33. Sabuda, Matt. (WBFO Sports Commentator) in discussion with the author. Aug. 15, 2018

34. Graham, Tim. (former Buffalo News sports reporter, senior writer at The Athletic) in discussion with the author. Feb. 25, 2019.

35. Graham, Tim. (Feb. 25, 2019).

36. Ostrander, Chris. (sportswriter, Two in the Box.com) in discussion with the author. Aug. 14, 2018.

37. Graham, Tim. (Feb. 25, 2019).

CHAPTER FOUR NOTES

1. Weiner, Evan. "Bud Adams and the Foolish Club." The Sport Digest.com. Oct. 22, 2013. Accessed Sept.12, 2018. http://thesportdigest.com/2013/10/bud-adams-and-the-foolish-club/

2. Weiner, Evan. (Oct. 22, 2013).

3. Weiner, Evan. (Oct. 22, 2013).

4. Weiner, Evan. (Oct. 22, 2013).

5. Weiner, Evan. (Oct. 22, 2013).

6. Weiner, Evan. (Oct. 22, 2013).

7. DeLamierelleure, Joe and Benson, Michael. "Chapter. 1: Showing Up." In Joe D.'s Tales of the Buffalo Bills. Champaign, IL: Sports Publishing, 2007. 5-6.

8. Gehman, Jim. "Introduction." In Then Levy Said to Kelly: The Best Buffalo Bills Stories Ever Told. Chicago: Triumph Books, 2008. Xvii.

9. Pitoniak, Scott. "Introduction." In The Good, the Bad, the Ugly Buffalo Bills. Chicago: Triumph Books, 2007. Xv.

10. Pitoniak, Scott. (2007). Xv.

11. Pitoniak, Scott. (2007). Xv.

12. Pitoniak, Scott. (2007). Xv.

13. Pitoniak, Scott. (2007). Xv.

14. Pitoniak, Scott. "Introduction." In The Good, the Bad, the Ugly Buffalo Bills. Chicago: Triumph Books, 2007. Xvi.

15. Pitoniak, Scott. (2007). Xvi.

16. Pitoniak, Scott. (2007). Xvi.

17. Morrison, Jim. "The American Football League's Foolish Club." Smithsonian. com. Jan. 14, 2010. Accessed Sept. 12, 2018. https://www.smithsonianmag. com/history/the-american-football-leagues-foolish-club-5340540/"Copyright 2010 Smithsonian Institution. Reprinted with permission from Smithsonian Enterprises. All rights reserved. Reproduction in any medium is strictly prohibited without permission from Smithsonian magazine."

18. Morrison, Jim. (Jan. 14, 2010).

19. Pitoniak, Scott. "Introduction." In The Good, the Bad, the Ugly Buffalo Bills. Chicago: Triumph Books, 2007. Xvii.

20. Morrison, Jim. (Jan. 14, 2010).

21. Miller, Jeffrey (author, Buffalo Bills historian) in discussion with the author. July 19, 2018.

22. Graham, Tim. (former Buffalo News sports reporter, senior writer at The Athletic) in discussion with the author. Feb. 25, 2019.

23. Graham, Tim. (Feb. 25, 2019).

24. Mairoana, Sal. (author, Rochester Democrat and Chronicle sports reporter) in discussion with the author. July 9, 2018.

25. Northrop, Milt. (Buffalo News sports reporter) in discussion with the author. Mar. 11, 2019.

26. Northrop, Milt. (Mar. 11, 2019).

27. Northrop, Milt. (Mar. 11, 2019).

28. Sabuda, Matt. (WBFO Sports Commentator) in discussion with the author. Aug. 15, 2018

29. Ostrander, Chris. (sportswriter, Two in the Box.com) in discussion with the author. Aug. 14, 2018.

30. Pitoniak, Scott. "Introduction." In The Good, the Bad, the Ugly Buffalo Bills. Chicago: Triumph Books, 2007. Xvi.

31. Pitoniak, Scott. (2007). Xvi.

32. Pitoniak, Scott. "Introduction." In The Good, the Bad, the Ugly Buffalo Bills. Chicago: Triumph Books, 2007. Xviii.

33. Pitoniak, Scott. "Introduction." In The Good, the Bad, the Ugly Buffalo Bills. Chicago: Triumph Books, 2007. Xix.

34. Pitoniak, Scott. (2007). Xix.

CHAPTER FIVE NOTES

1. "Bison's History. The 1880s." Milb.com. Accessed Oct. 1, 2018. http://www.milb.com/content/page.jsp?sid=t422&ymd=20060119&content_id=38582&vkey=team4 See also, Early. "Buffalo Baseball Briefly." Mop-Up-Duty.com. Mar. 16, 2008. http://mopupduty.com/buffalo-baseball-briefly/, "Federal League." Baseball Reference.com. https://www.baseball-reference.com/bullpen/Federal_League

2. Gleason, Bucky. "How the Braves came to Buffalo-and why they left." The Buffalo News, Apr. 22, 2016. Accessed Oct. 1, 2018. https://buffalonews.com/2016/04/22/braves-came-buffalo-left/

3. Picard, C. "Hockey Before Helmets: The Bisons and Championship Hockey in Buffalo." Buffalo Spree. Oct. 8, 2008. 46-56.

4. Klein, J. "In Buffalo, Hockey Survives (Barely) in What Was the Broadway Auditorium." The New York Times. Feb. 15, 2012.

5. Picard, C. "Hockey Before Helmets: The Bisons and Championship Hockey in Buffalo." Buffalo Spree. Oct. 8, 2008. 46-56.

6. Yates, Brock. "Warts, Love and Dreams in Buffalo." Sports Illustrated. Jan. 20, 1969. Accessed Oct. 1, 2018. https://www.si.com/vault/1969/01/20/542599/warts-love-and-dreams-in-buffalo

7. Brewitt, Ross. "Chicago…You'll Never Get In." In A Spin of the Wheel: Birth of the Buffalo Sabres. New York: Vantage Press, 1975. 32.

8. Bill. "The Birth of the Franchise." Sabres Fans.com. June 20, 2011. Accessed Oct. 1, 2018. http://sabresfans.com/2011/06/20/the-birth-of-the-franchise/

9. Bill. (June 20, 2011).

10. Bill. (June 20, 2011).

11. Maiorana, Sal. "Procuring A Franchise." In 100 Things Sabres Fans Should Know & Do Before They Die. Chicago, Triumph Books, 2012. 64.

12. Wieland, Paul. "Introduction." In Then Perreault Said to Rico: The Best Buffalo Sabres Stories Ever Told. Chicago, Triumph Books, 2008. Xiii.

13. Fleming, Frank. "Buffalo Sabres (1970-Present)." Sports Encyclopedia.com. March 28, 2018. Accessed October 2, 2018. http://www.sportsecyclopedia.com/nhl/buffalo/sabres.html

14. Maiorana, Sal. "Remember the Aud." In 100 Things Sabres Fans Should Know & Do Before They Die. Chicago, Triumph Books, 2012. 117.

15. Maiorana, Sal. "Remember the Aud." In 100 Things Sabres Fans Should Know & Do Before They Die. Chicago, Triumph Books, 2012. 118.

16. Maiorana, Sal. (2012). 117.

17. Fleming, Frank. "Buffalo Sabres (1970-Present)." Sports Encyclopedia.com. March 28, 2018. Accessed October 2, 2018. http://www.sportsecyclopedia.com/nhl/buffalo/sabres.html

18. Miller, James. "The road to perdition for Adelphia." Chicago Tribune. August 3, 2002. Accessed October 3, 2018. http://www.chicagotribune.com/news/ct-xpm-2002-08-03-0208030185-story.html

19. Fleming, Frank. (Mar. 28, 2018).

20. Mairorana, Sal. "No Goal." In 100 Things Sabres Fans Should Know & Do Before They Die. Chicago, Triumph Books, 2012. 13.

21. Fleming, Frank. (Mar. 28, 2018).

22. Adams, Thomas. "Score! How Thomas Golisano turned around a nearly

bankrupt NHL franchise." Rochester Business Journal. November 30, 2007. Accessed October 3, 2018. https://rbj.net/2007/11/30/score-how-thomas-golisano-turned-around-a-nearly-bankrupt-nhl-franchise/

23. Adams, Thomas. (Nov. 30, 2007).

24. Adams, Thomas. (Nov. 30, 2007).

25. Adams, Thomas. (Nov. 30, 2007).

26. Fleming, Frank. (Mar. 28, 2018).

27. Maiorana, Sal. "Drury and Briere Bolt." In 100 Things Sabres Fans Should Know & Do Before They Die. Chicago, Triumph Books, 2012. 51.

28. Maiorana, Sal. "Drury and Briere Bolt." In 100 Things Sabres Fans Should Know & Do Before They Die. Chicago, Triumph Books, 2012. 52.

29. Baumer, Kevin. "Is Tom Golisano Looking To Sell The Sabres?" Business Insider.com. Nov. 29, 2010. Accessed Oct. 9, 2018. https://www.businessinsider.com/is-tom-golisano-looking-to-sell-the-sabres-2010-11

30. Baumer, Kevin. (Nov. 29, 2010).

31. Dupont, Kevin Paul. "They're Sold. Stamkos is as good as advertised." Boston.com. Nov. 28, 2010. Accessed Oct. 9, 2018. http://archive.boston.com/sports/hockey/articles/2010/11/28/theyre_sold_stamkos_is_as_good_as_advertised/?page=3 "From The Boston Globe. © [2010] Boston Globe Media Partners. All rights reserved. Used under license."

32. Maiorana, Sal. "Who is Kim Pegula? Five things to know about Bills, Sabres co-owner." Democrat and Chronicle. May 2, 2018. Accessed Oct. 9, 2018. https://www.democratandchronicle.com/story/sports/football/nfl/bills/2018/05/02/kim-pegula-buffalo-bills-owner-terry-nfl-pegula-sports-entertainment-sabres-nhl/571622002/

33. "#153 Terrence Pegula." Forbes.com. Accessed Oct. 9, 2018. https://www.forbes.com/profile/terrence-pegula/#2136ac373cc7

34. Maiorana, Sal. (May 2, 2018).

35. Pollock, Chuck. "Remember when Pegula was a local hockey coach?" Ole-

an Times Herald. Feb. 22, 2016. Accessed Oct. 9, 2018. http://www.olean-timesherald.com/sports/columnists/remember-when-pegula-was-a-local-hockey-coach/article_b369f874-d847-11e5-b387-67e32cba2312.html

36. Kovach, Wayne. "Terry Pegula: A Fracking Billionaire." Your Energy Blog.com. Apr. 23, 2014. Accessed Oct. 9, 2018. http://www.yourenergyblog.com/terry-pegula-a-fracking-billionaire/

37. Kovach, Wayne. Apr. 23, 2014. Accessed Oct. 9, 2018. http://www.yourenergyblog.com/terry-pegula-a-fracking-billionaire/

38. Hughes, Travis. "Buffalo Sabres Announce Sale of Team to Terry Pegula." SB Nation.com. Feb. 1, 2011. Accessed Oct. 9, 2018. https://www.sbnation.com/nhl/2011/2/1/1968443/buffalo-sabres-sale-announcement-terry-pegula-tom-golisano

39. Bluedevil. "Mo Money, No Problems: Golisano's Sabres Investment Beat S&P, M&T and Paychex." Buffalo Rising.com. Feb. 3, 2011. Accessed Oct. 9, 2018. https://www.buffalorising.com/2011/02/golisano-as-investor-sabres-beat-sp-mt-and-paychex/

40. Adams, Thomas. (Nov. 30, 2007).

41. Vogl, John. "Destination: The Stanley Cup. Pegula Leaves No Doubt. Sabres' owner arrives with championship goal." The Buffalo News. Feb. 23, 2011. A2.

42. Vogl, John. (Feb. 23, 2011). A2.

43. Vogl, John. (Feb. 23, 2011). A2.

44. Vogl, John. (Feb. 23, 2011). A1.

45. Sabuda, Matt. (WBFO Sports Commentator) in discussion with the author. Aug. 15, 2018.

46. Graham, Tim. (former Buffalo News sports reporter, senior writer at The Athletic) in discussion with the author. Feb. 25, 2019.

47. Graham, Tim. (Feb. 25, 2019).

48. Maioana, Sal. (author, Rochester Democrat and Chronicle sports reporter) in discussion with the author. July 9, 2018.

49. Ostrander, Chris. (sportswriter, Two in the Box.com) in discussion with the author. Aug. 14, 2018.

50. Wieland, Paul. (author and former Sabres Public Relations Director) in discussion with the author. July 20, 2018.

51. Krieger, John. (sportswriter, Hockey Central.com) in discussion with the author. Oct. 13, 2018.

52. Graham, Tim. (Feb. 25, 2019).

53. Maiorana, Sal. "Dedication." In 100 Things Sabres Fans Should Know & Do Before They Die. Chicago, Triumph Books, 2012.

Chapter Six Notes

1. "History of the Penguins. 1980s" People.Cs.Pitt.edu. Accessed Oct. 13,2018. https://people.cs.pitt.edu/~mehmud/cs134-2084/projects/Team6/80s.html

2. Angotti, Louis F. (former Pittsburgh Penguins head coach) in correspondence with the author. June 18, 2020.

3. Finder, Chuck. "Finder: Lessons can be learned from Angotti and 1984." Pittsburgh Post-Gazette. Mar. 28, 2004. Accessed July 1, 2020. https://www.post-gazette.com/sports/chuck-finder/2004/03/28/Finder-Lessons-can-be-learned-from-Angotti-and-1984/stories/200403280235

4. Starkey, Joe. "Starkey: Remembering a long-forgotten Penguins hero." Trib Live.com. June 23, 2016. Accessed Oct. 13, 2018. https://archive.triblive.com/sports/penguins/starkey-remembering-a-long-forgotten-penguins-hero/

5. Angotti, Louis F. (June 18, 2020).

6. Angotti, Louis F. (June 18, 2020).

7. Politi, Steve. "Tanking in the NBA? Meet the hockey GM who refused to do it." NJ.com. Oct. 31, 2013. Accessed Oct. 13, 2018. https://www.nj.com/devils/index.ssf/2013/10/tanking_a_season_here_is_one_proud_gm_who_said_no_tanks.html. Reprinted courtesy of Steve Politi, NJ.com.

8. Andrew. "Tanks for the Memories: A Long History of the Worst Kept Secret in

Hockey." Welcome To Your Karlsson Years.com. Feb. 24, 2016. Accessed Oct. 13, 2018. https://welcometoyourkarlssonyears.com/2016/02/24/tanks-for-the-memories-a-long-history-of-the-worst-kept-secret-in-hockey-part-1/

9. Politi, Steve. (Oct. 31, 2013).

10. Starkey, Joe. (June 23, 2016).

11. Andrew. (Feb. 24, 2016).

12. "Eddie Johnston." Wikepedia.com. May 28, 2018. Accessed Oct. 13, 2018.

13. Ryndak, Chris. "Sabres relieve Ruff of coaching duties, name Rolston." NHL.com. Feb. 20, 2013. Accessed Oct. 15, 2018. https://www.nhl.com/news/sabres-relieve-ruff-of-coaching-duties-name-rolston/c-656635

14. Vogl, John. "Darcy's time a reign of error." The Buffalo News. Nov. 13, 2013.

15. Vogl, John. "Murray's straight talk sealed the deal." The Buffalo News. Jan. 9, 2014.

16. Dahlberg, Jeff. "The Sabres Tank for Eich." In Not Just Snow and Chicken Wings: Positive Stories About Buffalo's Rebirth." Seattle, Amazon Publishing, 2016. 35.

17. Harrington, Mike. "Sabres situation remains as clear as mud." The Buffalo News. Mar. 3, 2014.

18. Harrington, Mike. (Mar. 3, 2014).

19. Dahlberg, Jeff. (2016). 35.

20. Fleming, Frank. "Buffalo Sabres (1970-Present)." Sports Encyclopedia.com. Mar. 28, 2018. Accessed Oct. 15, 2018. http://www.sportsecyclopedia.com/nhl/buffalo/sabres.html

21. Dahlberg, Jeff. (2016). 35.

22. LeBrun, Pierre. "Tanking or trying? Sabres answer?" ESPN.com. January 22, 2015. Accessed Oct. 15, 2018. http://www.espn.com/nhl/story/_/id/12209280/nhl-accused-tanking-buffalo-sabres-insist-part-rebuild

23. LeBrun, Pierre. (Jan. 22, 2015).

24. Harrington, Mike. "Murray obviously relishing the status quo." The Buffalo News. Feb. 1, 2015.

25. Dahlberg, Jeff. "The Sabres Tank for Eich." In Not Just Snow and Chicken Wings: Positive Stories About Buffalo's Rebirth." Seattle, Amazon Publishing, 2016. 36.

26. Vogl, John. "Sabres notebook-Nolan wants Myers to be a building block." The Buffalo News. Feb. 4, 2015.

27. Harrington, Mike. (Feb. 1, 2015).

28. Gleason, Bucky. "Rooting for defeat brings a house divided." The Buffalo News. Mar. 27, 2015.

29. Gleason, Bucky. (Mar. 27, 2015).

30. Lenihan, Emily. "Do you want the Buffalo Sabres to tank?" Wivb.com. Mar. 30, 2015. Accessed Oct. 15, 2018. https://www.wivb.com/sports/buffalo-sabres/do-you-want-the-buffalo-sabres-to-tank/1108643252

31. Ray, Jay. "Sabres boost hopes of tankers." The Buffalo News. Mar. 27, 2015.

32. Dedominicis, Chad. "Sabres Future Decided in Less Than 5 Minutes." The Hockey Writers.com. Apr. 10, 2015. Accessed Oct. 15, 2018. https://thehockeywriters.com/sabres-future-decided-in-less-than-5-minutes/

33. Ryndak, Chris. "Sabres Locked Into Last Place With Loss to Blue Jackets." NHL.com. Apr.11, 2015. Accessed Oct. 15, 2018. https://www.nhl.com/sabres/news/sabres-locked-into-last-place-with-loss-to-blue-jackets/c-762569

34. Dahlberg, Jeff. "The Sabres Tank for Eich." In Not Just Snow and Chicken Wings: Positive Stories About Buffalo's Rebirth." Seattle, Amazon Publishing, 2016. 41.

35. Harrington, Mike. "Sabres probable pick won Hobey Baker award." The Buffalo News. Apr. 19, 2015.

36. Harrington, Mike. Apr. 19, 2015.

37. Harrington, Mike. Apr. 19, 2015.

38. Vogl, John. "Jackpot BU star calls selection, "a dream come true". The Buffalo News. June 27, 2015.

39. Vogl, John. (June 27, 2015).

40. "Jack Eichel." Hockey Reference.com. Accessed April 13, 2020. https://www.

hockey-reference.com/players/e/eicheja01.html

41. Sabuda, Matt. (WBFO sports commentator) in discussion with the author. Aug. 15, 2018.

42. Graham, Tim. (former Buffalo News sports reporter, senior writer at The Athletic) in discussion with the author. Feb. 25, 2019.

43. Graham, Tim. (Feb. 25, 2019).

44. Maiorana, Sal. (author, Rochester Democrat and Chronicle sports reporter) in discussion with the author. July 9, 2018.

45. Maiorana, Sal. (July 9, 2018).

46. Wieland, Paul. (author and former Sabres Public Relations Director) in discussion with the author. July 20, 2018.

47. Ostrander, Chris. (sportswriter, Two in the Box.com) in discussion with the author. Aug. 14, 2018.

48. Ostrander, Chris. (Aug. 14, 2018).

49. Krieger, John. (sportswriter, Hockey Central.com) in discussion with the author. Oct. 13, 2018.

CHAPTER SEVEN NOTES

1. "1998-99 Buffalo Sabres Roster and Statistics." Hockey Reference.com. Oct. 18, 2018. Accessed Oct. 18, 2018. https://www.hockey-reference.com/teams/BUF/1999.html

2. Zielonka, Zachary. "1999 Stanley Cup Finals Remix: The State of the Sabres." Die By the Blade.com. June 15, 2009. Accessed Oct. 18, 2018. https://www.diebytheblade.com/2009/6/15/910412/1999-cup-finals-remix-the-state-of

3. "1999 Stanley Cup Playoffs." Wikepedia. May 16, 2018. Accessed Oct. 18, 2018. https://en.wikipedia.org/wiki/1999_Stanley_Cup_playoffs#(2)_Ottawa_Senators_vs._(7)_Buffalo_Sabres

4. "1999 Stanley Cup Playoffs." (May 16, 2018).

5. "1999 Stanley Cup Playoffs." (May 16, 2018).

6. "1999 Stanley Cup Playoffs." (May 16, 2018).

7. Maiorana, Sal. "The 1999 Finals." In 100 Things Sabres Fans Must Know & Do Before They Die. Chicago, Triumph Books, 2012. 25-26.

8. Maiorana, Sal. (2012). 27.

9. "1998-99 Dallas Stars season." Wikepedia. Oct. 8, 2018. Accessed Oct. 18, 2018. https://en.wikipedia.org/wiki/1998%E2%80%9399_Dallas_Stars_season

10. Lansky, Steve. "1999 Stanley Cup Championship Series." 2010. Acessed Oct.18, 2018. http://bigmouthsports.com/wp-content/uploads/2014/10/1999-Stanley-Cup-Playoff-boxscores-DAL.pdf

11. Maiorana, Sal. "The 1999 Finals." In 100 Things Sabres Fans Must Know & Do Before They Die. Chicago, Triumph Books, 2012. 27.

12. Lansky, Steve. (2010).

13. Maiorana, Sal. "No Goal." In 100 Things Sabres Fans Must Know and Do Before They Die. Chicago, Triumph Books, 2012. 14-16.

14. Brand, J. David. "Worst Buffalo Sports Moment #2-No Goal." UB Bull Run. com. August 6, 2014. Accessed October 19, 2018. https://www.ubbullrun. com/2014/8/6/5801764/buffalo-worst-sports-moments-no-goal-sabres-stars-stanley-cup-final

15. Maiorana, Sal. "No Goal." In 100 Things Sabres Fans Must Know & Do Before They Die. Chicago, Triumph Books, 2012. 16.

16. Maiorana, Sal. (2012). 16.

17. Maiorana, Sal. "No Goal." In 100 Things Sabres Fans Must Know & Do Before They Die. Chicago, Triumph Books, 2012. 14.

18. Maiorana, Sal. (2012). 14.

19. Barr, Josh. "Stanley Cup Ends In Controversy." The Washington Post. June 21, 1999. Accessed October 19, 2018. http://www.washingtonpost.com/wp-srv/sports/nhl/longterm/1999/stanleycup/articles/nhl21.htm

20. Barr, Josh. (June 21, 1999).

21. Maiorana, Sal. (2012). 14.

22. Farber, Michael. "The Bitter End: A Dubious Goal That Gave the Stars the Stanley Cup Over the Sabres Tarnished What Had Been the Best Final Series in Years." Sports Illustrated.com. June 28, 1999. Accessed Oct. 19, 2018. https://www.si.com/vault/1999/06/28/262998/the-bitter-end-a-dubious-goal-that-gave-the-stars-the-stanley-cup-over-the-sabres-tarnished-what-had-been-the-best-final-series-in-years. "Reprinted courtesy of SPORTS ILLUSTRATED: "The Bitter End: A Dubious Goal That Gave the Stars the Stanley Cup Tarnished What Had Been the Best Final Series in Years" by Michael Farber, June 28, 1999 Copyright © 2020. ABG-SI. LLC. All rights reserved"

23. Farber, Michael. (June 28, 1999). "Reprinted courtesy of SPORTS ILLUSTRATED: "The Bitter End: A Dubious Goal That Gave the Stars the Stanley Cup Tarnished What Had Been the Best Final Series in Years" by Michael Farber, June 28, 1999 Copyright © 2020. ABG-SI. LLC. All rights reserved"

24. Farber, Michael. (June 28, 1999). "Reprinted courtesy of SPORTS ILLUSTRATED: "The Bitter End: A Dubious Goal That Gave the Stars the Stanley Cup Tarnished What Had Been the Best Final Series in Years" by Michael Farber, June 28, 1999 Copyright © 2020. ABG-SI. LLC. All rights reserved"

25. Schultz, Randy. "No Goal." In Dominik Hasek: The Dominator." New York, Sports Publishing, 2002. 78.

26. Maiorana, Sal. (2012). 16.

27. Wieland, Paul. (author and former Sabres Public Relations Director) in discussion with the author. July 20, 2018.

28. Wieland, Paul. (July 20, 2018).

29. Graham, Tim. (former Buffalo News sports reporter, senior writer at The Athletic) in discussion with the author. Feb. 25, 2019.

30. Graham, Tim. (Feb. 25, 2019).

31. Ostrander, Chris. (sportswriter, Two in the Box.com) in discussion with the author. Aug. 14, 2018.

32. Ostrander, Chris. (Aug. 14, 2018).

33. Sabuda, Matt. (WBFO Sports Commentator) in discussion with the author. Aug. 15, 2018.

34. Brewitt, Ross. (author) in discussion with the author. July 7, 2018.

35. Krieger, John. (sportswriter, Hockey Central.com) in discussion with the author. Oct. 13, 2018.

CHAPTER EIGHT NOTES

1. Klein, Cutler. "From six teams to 31: History of NHL expansion." NHL.com. June 22, 2016. Accessed Oct. 19, 2018. https://www.nhl.com/news/nhl-expansion-history/c-281005106

2. Wieland, Paul. "The Beginning." In Then Perreault Said to Rico: The Best Buffalo Sabres Stories Ever Told. Chicago, Triumph, 2008. 7.

3. Wieland, Paul. (2008). 7.

4. Wieland, Paul. (author and former Sabres Public Relations Director) in discussion with the author. July 20, 2018.

5. Brewitt, Ross. (author) in discussion with the author. July 7, 2018.

6. Wieland, Paul. (2008). 7.

7. Brewitt, Ross. (July 7, 2018).

8. Maiorana, Sal. "Can Anybody Around Here Play This Game?" In Thank You Sabres: Memories of the 1972-73 Season. Coal Valley, IL, Quality Sports Publications, 1997. 26-27.

9. Maiorana, Sal. "The Sophomore Jinx" In Thank You Sabres: Memories of the 1972-73 Season. Coal Valley, IL, Quality Sports Publications, 1997. 29-30.

10. Maiorana, Sal. "The Sophomore Jinx" In Thank You Sabres: Memories of the 1972-73 Season. Coal Valley, IL, Quality Sports Publications, 1997. 37.

11. Fleming, Frank. "Buffalo Sabres (1970-Present)." Sports Encyclopedia.com. Mar. 28, 2018. Accessed October 20, 2018. http://www.sportsecyclopedia.com/nhl/buffalo/sabres.html

12. Maiorana, Sal. "October: They Might Never Lose" In Thank You Sabres: Memories of the 1972-73 Season. Coal Valley, IL, Quality Sports Publications,

1997. 71.

13. Fleming, Frank. (Mar. 28, 2018).

14. Fleming, Frank. (Mar. 28, 2018).

15. Fleming, Frank. (Mar. 28, 2018).

16. Fleming, Frank. (Mar. 28, 2018).

17. Fleming, Frank. (Mar. 28, 2018).

18. Maiorana, Sal. "The Saga of Perreault's Retirement." In 100 Things Sabres Fans Should Know & Do Before They Die. Chicago, Triumph Books, 2012. 170.

19. Maiorana, Sal. (2012). 170.

20. Maiorana, Sal. (2012). 170.

21. Maiorana, Sal. "The Saga of Perreault's Retirement." In 100 Things Sabres Fans Should Know & Do Before They Die. Chicago, Triumph Books, 2012. 171.

22. Hoppe, Bill. "Flashback: Terry Pegula's emotional purchase of Sabres." Buffalo Hockey Beat.com. Sept. 9, 2014. Accessed Oct. 22, 2018. http://www.buffalo-hockeybeat.com/flashback-terry-pegulas-emotional-purchase-of-sabres/

23. Hoppe, Bill. (Sept. 9, 2014).

24. "Sabres unveil statue of French Connection line." NHL.com. Oct. 13, 2012. Accessed Oct. 31, 2018. https://www.nhl.com/news/sabres-unveil-statue-of-french-connection-line/c-643369

25. Olesky, David. "What if the Sabres Did Not Draft Gilbert Perreault?" Die By the Blade.com. May 5, 2010. Accessed Oct. 22, 2018. https://www.diebytheb-lade.com/2010/5/5/1459185/what-if-the-sabres-did-not-draft

26. Wieland, Paul. (author and former Sabres Public Relations Director) in discussion with the author. July 20, 2018.

27. Wieland, Paul. (July 20, 2018).

28. Maiorana, Sal. (author, Rochester Democrat and Chronicle sports reporter) in discussion with the author. July 9, 2018.

29. Maiorana, Sal. (July 9, 2018).

30. Ostrander, Chris. (sportswriter, Two in the Box.com) in discussion with the

author. Aug. 14, 2018.

31. Sabuda, Matt. (WBFO Sports Commentator) in discussion with the author. Aug. 15, 2018.

32. Krieger, John. (sportswriter, Hockey Central.com) in discussion with the author. Oct. 13, 2018.

33. Krieger, John. (Oct. 13, 2018).

CHAPTER NINE NOTES

1. "Managers of the Buffalo Bisons (1879-18885)." Baseball Almanac.com. 2018. Accessed October 23, 2018. http://www.baseball-almanac.com/mgrtmbb9.shtml

2. Violanti, Anthony. "Rising From The Dead." In Miracle in Buffalo: How the Dream of Baseball Revived a City." New York, St. Martin's Press, 1991. 11.

3. "Bisons History. The 1880's." Milb.com. 2018. Accessed Oct. 23, 2018. http://www.milb.com/content/page.jsp?sid=t422&ymd=20060119&content_id=38582&vkey=team4

4. "Bisons History. The 1880's." (2018).

5. Dahlberg, Jeff. "Terry Pegula and some loyal fans keep the Bills in Buffalo." In Not Just Snow and Chicken Wings: Positive Stories About Buffalo's Rebirth." Seattle, Amazon Publishing, 2016. 8-9.

6. Violanti, Anthony. (1991). 11.

7. Violanti, Anthony. (1991). 11. Quotes from MIRACLE IN BUFFALO: HOW THE DREAM OF BASEBALL REVIVED A CITY. Copyright © 1991 by Anthony Violanti. Reprinted by permission of St. Martin's Press. All Rights Reserved.

8. Violanti, Anthony. (1991). 11. Quotes from MIRACLE IN BUFFALO: HOW THE DREAM OF BASEBALL REVIVED A CITY. Copyright © 1991 by Anthony Violanti. Reprinted by permission of St. Martin's Press. All Rights Reserved.

9. "Bisons History. The 1950s." Milb.com. 2018. Accessed Oct. 23, 2018. http://

www.milb.com/content/page.jsp?sid=t422&ymd=20060119&content_id=38582&vkey=team4

10. Violanti, Anthony. "Rising From The Dead." In Miracle in Buffalo: How the Dream of Baseball Revived a City." New York, St. Martin's Press, 1991. 13.

11. Dahlberg, Jeff. "Terry Pegula and some loyal fans keep the Bills in Buffalo." In Not Just Snow and Chicken Wings: Positive Stories About Buffalo's Rebirth." Seattle, Amazon Publishing, 2016. 13.

12. "Bisons History. The 1960s." Milb.com. 2018. Accessed Oct. 23, 2018. http://www.milb.com/content/page.jsp?sid=t422&ymd=20060119&content_id=38582&vkey=team4

13. Byrnes, Mark. "They Built It, But the MLB never came." City Lab.com. July 10, 2012. Accessed Oct. 24, 2018. https://www.citylab.com/life/2012/07/they-built-it-mlb-never-came/2509/

14. Violanti, Anthony. "Rising From The Dead." In Miracle in Buffalo: How the Dream of Baseball Revived a City." New York, St. Martin's Press, 1991. 8. Quotes from MIRACLE IN BUFFALO: HOW THE DREAM OF BASEBALL REVIVED A CITY. Copyright © 1991 by Anthony Violanti. Reprinted by permission of St. Martin's Press. All Rights Reserved.

15. "Bisons History. The 1970s." Milb.com. 2018. Accessed Oct. 23, 2018. http://www.milb.com/content/page.jsp?sid=t422&ymd=20060119&content_id=38582&vkey=team4

16. Violanti, Anthony. "Irish Jimmy." In Miracle in Buffalo: How the Dream of Baseball Revived a City." New York, St. Martin's Press, 1991. 33. Quotes from MIRACLE IN BUFFALO: HOW THE DREAM OF BASEBALL REVIVED A CITY. Copyright © 1991 by Anthony Violanti. Reprinted by permission of St. Martin's Press. All Rights Reserved.

17. Violanti, Anthony. "Irish Jimmy." In Miracle in Buffalo: How the Dream of Baseball Revived a City." New York, St. Martin's Press, 1991. 35 Quotes from MIRACLE IN BUFFALO: HOW THE DREAM OF BASEBALL REVIVED A

CITY. Copyright © 1991 by Anthony Violanti. Reprinted by permission of St. Martin's Press. All Rights Reserved.

18. Violanti, Anthony. "Irish Jimmy." In Miracle in Buffalo: How the Dream of Baseball Revived a City." New York, St. Martin's Press, 1991. 35-37.

19. Violanti, Anthony. "Irish Jimmy." In Miracle in Buffalo: How the Dream of Baseball Revived a City." New York, St. Martin's Press, 1991. 37. Quotes from MIRACLE IN BUFFALO: HOW THE DREAM OF BASEBALL REVIVED A CITY. Copyright © 1991 by Anthony Violanti. Reprinted by permission of St. Martin's Press. All Rights Reserved.

20. Violanti, Anthony. (1991). 37. Quotes from MIRACLE IN BUFFALO: HOW THE DREAM OF BASEBALL REVIVED A CITY. Copyright © 1991 by Anthony Violanti. Reprinted by permission of St. Martin's Press. All Rights Reserved.

21. Violanti, Anthony. "Irish Jimmy." In Miracle in Buffalo: How the Dream of Baseball Revived a City." New York, St. Martin's Press, 1991. 38. Quotes from MIRACLE IN BUFFALO: HOW THE DREAM OF BASEBALL REVIVED A CITY. Copyright © 1991 by Anthony Violanti. Reprinted by permission of St. Martin's Press. All Rights Reserved.

22. Violanti, Anthony. "Irish Jimmy." In Miracle in Buffalo: How the Dream of Baseball Revived a City." New York, St. Martin's Press, 1991. 40. Quotes from MIRACLE IN BUFFALO: HOW THE DREAM OF BASEBALL REVIVED A CITY. Copyright © 1991 by Anthony Violanti. Reprinted by permission of St. Martin's Press. All Rights Reserved.

23. Violanti, Anthony. "Irish Jimmy." In Miracle in Buffalo: How the Dream of Baseball Revived a City." New York, St. Martin's Press, 1991. 41. Quotes from MIRACLE IN BUFFALO: HOW THE DREAM OF BASEBALL REVIVED A CITY. Copyright © 1991 by Anthony Violanti. Reprinted by permission of St. Martin's Press. All Rights Reserved.

24. Violanti, Anthony. (1991). 44. Quotes from MIRACLE IN BUFFALO: HOW

THE DREAM OF BASEBALL REVIVED A CITY. Copyright © 1991 by Anthony Violanti. Reprinted by permission of St. Martin's Press. All Rights Reserved.

25. Violanti, Anthony. (1991). 44. Quotes from MIRACLE IN BUFFALO: HOW THE DREAM OF BASEBALL REVIVED A CITY. Copyright © 1991 by Anthony Violanti. Reprinted by permission of St. Martin's Press. All Rights Reserved.

26. Violanti, Anthony. (1991). 45. Quotes from MIRACLE IN BUFFALO: HOW THE DREAM OF BASEBALL REVIVED A CITY. Copyright © 1991 by Anthony Violanti. Reprinted by permission of St. Martin's Press. All Rights Reserved.

27. Violanti, Anthony. (1991). 45. Quotes from MIRACLE IN BUFFALO: HOW THE DREAM OF BASEBALL REVIVED A CITY. Copyright © 1991 by Anthony Violanti. Reprinted by permission of St. Martin's Press. All Rights Reserved.

28. Violanti, Anthony. (1991). 45. Quotes from MIRACLE IN BUFFALO: HOW THE DREAM OF BASEBALL REVIVED A CITY. Copyright © 1991 by Anthony Violanti. Reprinted by permission of St. Martin's Press. All Rights Reserved.

29. Byrnes, Mark. (July 10, 2012).

30. Violanti, Anthony. "Cutting A Diamond." In Miracle in Buffalo: How the Dream of Baseball Revived a City." New York, St. Martin's Press, 1991. 150 Quotes from MIRACLE IN BUFFALO: HOW THE DREAM OF BASEBALL REVIVED A CITY. Copyright © 1991 by Anthony Violanti. Reprinted by permission of St. Martin's Press. All Rights Reserved.

31. Violanti, Anthony. "Cutting A Diamond." In Miracle in Buffalo: How the Dream of Baseball Revived a City." New York, St. Martin's Press, 1991. 150-152.

32. Violanti, Anthony. "Cutting A Diamond." In Miracle in Buffalo: How the

Dream of Baseball Revived a City." New York, St. Martin's Press, 1991. 161. Quotes from MIRACLE IN BUFFALO: HOW THE DREAM OF BASEBALL REVIVED A CITY. Copyright © 1991 by Anthony Violanti. Reprinted by permission of St. Martin's Press. All Rights Reserved.

33. Byrnes, Mark. (July 10, 2012).

34. Violanti, Anthony. "Inside Baseball." In Miracle in Buffalo: How the Dream of Baseball Revived a City." New York, St. Martin's Press, 1991. 234. Quotes from MIRACLE IN BUFFALO: HOW THE DREAM OF BASEBALL REVIVED A CITY. Copyright © 1991 by Anthony Violanti. Reprinted by permission of St. Martin's Press. All Rights Reserved.

35. Violanti, Anthony. (1991). 234. Quotes from MIRACLE IN BUFFALO: HOW THE DREAM OF BASEBALL REVIVED A CITY. Copyright © 1991 by Anthony Violanti. Reprinted by permission of St. Martin's Press. All Rights Reserved.

36. Byrnes, Mark. (July 10, 2012).

37. Northrop, Milt. (Buffalo News sports reporter) in discussion with the author. Mar. 11, 2019.

38. Northrop, Milt. (Mar. 11, 2019).

39. Northrop, Milt. (Mar. 11, 2019).

40. Maiorana, Sal. (author, Rochester Democrat and Chronicle sports beat reporter) in discussion with the author. July 9, 2018.

41. Maiorana, Sal. (July 9, 2018).

42. Ostrander, Chris. (sportswriter, Two in the Box.com) in discussion with the author. Aug. 14, 2018.

43. Sabuda, Matt. (WBFO Sports Commentator) in discussion with the author. Aug. 15, 2018.

Chapter Ten Notes

1. Gleason, Bucky. "How the Braves came to Buffalo-and why they left." The

Buffalo News, Apr. 22, 2016. Accessed Oct. 29, 2018. https://buffalonews. com/2016/04/22/braves-came-buffalo-left/

2. "National Basketball Association." Wikepedia.com. Oct. 29, 2018. Accessed Oct. 29, 2018. https://en.wikipedia.org/wiki/National_Basketball_Association

3. Wendel, Tim. "Season 1: 1970-71." In Buffalo, Home of the Braves." Traverse City, MI, Sun Bear Press, 2009. 12.

4. Gleason, Bucky. (Apr. 22, 2016).

5. Gleason, Bucky. (Apr. 22, 2016).

6. Wendel, Tim. "Season 1: 1970-71." In Buffalo, Home of the Braves." Traverse City, MI, Sun Bear Press, 2009. 14, 19.

7. Gleason, Bucky. (Apr. 22, 2016).

8. Wendel, Tim. "Season 1: 1970-71." In Buffalo, Home of the Braves." Traverse City, MI, Sun Bear Press, 2009. 23.

9. "Buffalo Braves Record." NBA.com. Accessed October 31, 2018. https://www. nba.com/clippers/history/braves_stats.html

10. Wendel, Tim. "Season 2: 1971-72." In Buffalo, Home of the Braves." Traverse City, MI, Sun Bear Press, 2009. 34.

11. Wendel, Tim. "Season 2: 1971-72." In Buffalo, Home of the Braves." Traverse City, MI, Sun Bear Press, 2009. 36, 37.

12. Wendel, Tim. "Season 2: 1971-72." In Buffalo, Home of the Braves." Traverse City, MI, Sun Bear Press, 2009. 45.

13. Wendel, Tim. "Season 2: 1971-72." In Buffalo, Home of the Braves." Traverse City, MI, Sun Bear Press, 2009. 46.

14. "Buffalo Braves Record." (2018)

15. Wendel, Tim. (2009). 46-47.

16. Wendel, Tim. "Season 2: 1971-72." In Buffalo, Home of the Braves." Traverse City, MI, Sun Bear Press, 2009. 47, 50.

17. Wendel, Tim. "Season 3: 1972-73." In Buffalo, Home of the Braves." Traverse

City, MI, Sun Bear Press, 2009. 58.

18. Wendel, Tim. "Season 3: 1972-73." In Buffalo, Home of the Braves." Traverse City, MI, Sun Bear Press, 2009. 61, 64.

19. Wendel, Tim. "Season 3: 1972-73." In Buffalo, Home of the Braves." Traverse City, MI, Sun Bear Press, 2009. 65.

20. Wendel, Tim. "Season 4: 1973-74." In Buffalo, Home of the Braves." Traverse City, MI, Sun Bear Press, 2009. 80.

21. Buffalo Braves Record." (2018)

22. Wendel, Tim. "Season 3: 1972-73." In Buffalo, Home of the Braves." Traverse City, MI, Sun Bear Press, 2009. 74.

23. Northrop, Milt. (Buffalo News sports reporter) in discussion with the author. Mar. 11, 2019.

24. Buffalo Braves Record." (2018)

25. Wendel, Tim. "Season 5: 1974-75." In Buffalo, Home of the Braves." Traverse City, MI, Sun Bear Press, 2009. 130-136.

26. Buffalo Braves Record." (2018)

27. Wendel, Tim. "Season 6: 1975-76." In Buffalo, Home of the Braves." Traverse City, MI, Sun Bear Press, 2009. 151-160.

28. Wendel, Tim. "Season 6: 1975-76." In Buffalo, Home of the Braves." Traverse City, MI, Sun Bear Press, 2009. 160.

29. Wendel, Tim. "Season 6: 1975-76." In Buffalo, Home of the Braves." Traverse City, MI, Sun Bear Press, 2009. 161-162.

30. Wendel, Tim. "Season 6: 1975-76." In Buffalo, Home of the Braves." Traverse City, MI, Sun Bear Press, 2009. 162.

31. Wendel, Tim. "Season 7: 1976-77." In Buffalo, Home of the Braves." Traverse City, MI, Sun Bear Press, 2009. 166.

32. Wendel, Tim. "Season 7: 1976-77." In Buffalo, Home of the Braves." Traverse City, MI, Sun Bear Press, 2009. 166-170.

33. Wendel, Tim. "Season 7: 1976-77." In Buffalo, Home of the Braves." Traverse

City, MI, Sun Bear Press, 2009. 170.

34. Wendel, Tim. (2009). 170.

35. Wendel, Tim. "Season 7: 1976-77." In Buffalo, Home of the Braves." Traverse City, MI, Sun Bear Press, 2009. 171.

36. Wendel, Tim. "Season 7: 1976-77." In Buffalo, Home of the Braves." Traverse City, MI, Sun Bear Press, 2009. 171-175.

37. Wendel, Tim. "Season 7: 1976-77." In Buffalo, Home of the Braves." Traverse City, MI, Sun Bear Press, 2009. 175.

38. Wendel, Tim. "Season 7: 1976-77." In Buffalo, Home of the Braves." Traverse City, MI, Sun Bear Press, 2009. 176.

39. Wendel, Tim. "Season 7: 1976-77." In Buffalo, Home of the Braves." Traverse City, MI, Sun Bear Press, 2009. 177.

40. Wendel, Tim. "Season 7: 1976-77." In Buffalo, Home of the Braves." Traverse City, MI, Sun Bear Press, 2009. 180.

41. Buffalo Braves Record." (2018)

42. Wendel, Tim. "Season 7: 1976-77." In Buffalo, Home of the Braves." Traverse City, MI, Sun Bear Press, 2009. 186-188.

43. Buffalo Braves Record." (2018)

44. Wendel, Tim. "Season 8: 1977-78." In Buffalo, Home of the Braves." Traverse City, MI, Sun Bear Press, 2009. 209-212.

45. Sabuda, Matt. (WBFO Sports Commentator) in discussion with the author. Aug. 15, 2018.

46. Ostrander, Chris. (sportswriter, Two in the Box.com) in discussion with the author. Aug. 14, 2018.

47. Northrop, Milt. (Buffalo News sports reporter) in discussion with the author. Mar. 11, 2019.

48. Northrop, Milt. (Mar. 11, 2019).

49. Gleason, Bucky. (Apr. 22, 2016).

50. Northrop, Milt. (Mar. 11, 2019).

51. Maiorana, Sal. (author, Rochester Democrat and Chronicle sports reporter) in discussion with the author. July 9, 2018.

52. Northrop, Milt. (Mar. 11, 2019).

53. Maiorana, Sal. (July 9, 2018).

54. Northrop, Milt. (Mar. 11, 2019).

55. Northrop, Milt. (Mar. 11, 2019).

56. Wendel, Tim. (author, Buffalo Home of the Braves) in discussion with the author. Aug. 22, 2018.

57. Northrop, Milt. (Mar. 11, 2019).

58. Wendel, Tim. (Aug. 22, 2018).

59. Maiorana, Sal. (July 9, 2018).

60. Wendel, Tim. (Aug. 22, 2018).

61. Wendel, Tim. (Aug. 22, 2018).

62. Wendel, Tim. (Aug. 22, 2018).

THANKS

I had a lot of help and encouragement from many different people. Writing a book is a group project, and I couldn't have done this alone. Special thanks go to:

- Bruce Andriatch, assistant managing editor and Amy Yakawiak, Rights, Permissions & Reprints, The Buffalo News
- Louis F. Angotti, former head coach, Pittsburgh Penguins
- Gregg Brandon, EVP and general counsel and Kathryn D'Angelo, assistant general counsel, Buffalo Bills LLC
- Ross Brewitt, author of A Spin of the Wheel: Birth of the Buffalo Sabres
- Bob Busser, owner, Creative Vision Photography
- Mark Byrnes, author of "They Built It, but the MLB Never Came."
- Stacy Clark, director, Talent Negotiations & Rights and Clearances, NBC Universal
- Dr. John S. Dahlberg, Ph.D., chair/professor of communication, Canisius College
- Daniel DiLandro, SUNY Buffalo State archivist, special collections librarian
- Ralph Drew, Rights & Permissions, Los Angeles Times
- Jim Eckstrom, editor and Nichole Finnerty, circulation manager, Olean-Times Herald
- Vinessa Erminio, research editor, NJ Advance Media
- Mark Gompertz, group editorial director, Marissa Jones, accountant and Tony Lyons, president, Skyhorse Publishing, Inc.
- Tim Graham, former Buffalo News sports reporter and senior writer at The Athletic
- Natalie Hamilton, magazine permissions manager, Smithsonian Magazine
- Will Herman, assistant general counsel, Tegna, Inc. parent of WGRZ TV

- Mat Hooper, Stewart Kramer and Heather Osborne, PARS Int. Corp.
- Bonnie L. Jarrett, intellectual property counsel and Alexandra Smoczkiewicz, paralegal, National Football League
- Prem Kalliat, Director, Content Management Group at Sports Illustrated
- John Krieger, sportswriter at Hockey Central.com
- Jamie Lee, Licensing, Condé Nast
- Sal Maiorana, author and Rochester Democrat and Chronicle sports reporter
- Jeff Miller, author and Buffalo Bills historian
- Adam Motin, editorial director, Triumph Books
- Milt Northrop, Buffalo News sports reporter
- Chris Ostrander, sportswriter at Two in the Box.com
- Kevin O'Sullivan, AP Images
- Linda Parker, permissions staff, Pittsburgh Post-Gazette
- Rachel Pietrewicz, permissions assistant, Macmillan Publishing Group
- Mark Pogodzinski, owner, NFB Publishing
- Mark Preisler, EVP, Pegula Sports and Entertainment
- Kitty Ratcliffe, president, Explore St. Louis
- Tracy Rouch, director of public relations, St. Louis Post-Dispatch
- Matt Sabuda, sports commentator at WBFO
- Karen Schiffmacher, Product Sales, Audience Development and Subscriptions, Buffalo Business First
- David Schultz, director of content/audience, South Florida Sun Sentinel
- Jessica Sims, marketing & events coordinator, Rochester Business Journal
- Cynthia Van Ness, director of library & archives, The Buffalo History Museum
- Kathryn Walsh, intern, Hachette Book Group, Inc.
- Laura Watts, senior manager, Editorial Business Development, Shutterstock

- Chris Wendel, owner, Sun Bear Press and publisher of Buffalo Home of the Braves
- Tim Wendel, author of Buffalo: Home of the Braves
- Paul Wieland, author and former public relations director, Buffalo Sabres

ABOUT THE AUTHOR

Jeff Dahlberg is the author of *Not Just Snow and Chicken Wings: Positive Stories About Buffalo's Rebirth* and *We All Just Bought a Team: The Biggest What-Ifs in Buffalo Sports History*. He's also a freelance writer who specializes in promotional stories for new entrepreneurs and business startups. Jeff was born and raised in Western New York. A University at Buffalo and Second City Toronto graduate, he longs for the day when both the Bills win a Super Bowl and the Sabres win a Stanley Cup.